Eating & Drinking in

PARIS

·

French Menu Translator and Restaurant Guide

Andy Herbach

OPEN ROAD PUBLISHING

OPEN ROAD PUBLISHING

Your passport to the perfect trip!

Open Road Publishing
P.O. Box 284
Cold Spring Harbor, NY 11724

www.openroadguides.com

Seventh edition

Illustrations by Michael Dillon
Updated by Andy Herbach

Library of Congress Control No.
2014959136

ISBN: 978-1-59360-210-9

Contents

When you think of Paris, you may think of the Eiffel Tower, the Louvre or the Champs-Elysées. When we think of Paris, the first thing that comes to mind is food.

Of course, every traveler has a different set of desires and expectations: rest and relaxation, shopping, exploring, hiking, reading... For us, the making of a memorable vacation begins and ends with food.

Beyond the simple pleasures of eating, dining in a foreign country gives you an insight into the soul of its people. It's a glimpse of their customs, their likes and dislikes, their foibles, their accomplishments. It puts you in contact with local culture.

If you love to travel as we do, you know the importance of a good guide. Dining, like traveling, requires the same. A good guide can make the difference between a memorable evening and a nightmare or maybe just a dull one, but who wants a dull evening when they're on vacation? There is nothing worse than hiking all over a city looking for a good place to eat dinner, finding nothing, in near panic settling for whatever comes along next, having a lousy meal, then, upon leaving, discovering what looks like the best restaurant in the world right around the corner. Believe us, it happens all the time.

The restaurant-guide portion of our book is a list of some of our favorite places in Paris, and the menu-translator section will help you find your way around a menu written in French. It gives you the freedom to fearlessly enter places you might never have entered before and order a dinner without pointing or hand waving.

Eating & Drinking in Paris isn't so much about food and wine. It's really about easing the process of ordering food and having a good time – or at least not a stressful time – doing it. Our guide was created for the not-so-daring traveler who wants to enjoy and experience authentic cuisine and know what he or she is eating.

No other city in the world has a greater number of places to eat per square mile than Paris.
Nowhere else can you find the variety, the
charm, the sheer joy and celebration of food.
And nowhere else can you be more intimidated
trying to get fed. Parisians observe all kinds
of decorum about their food. They have many,
many types of eating establishments which
to us is confusing. What's wrong with calling
them all restaurants? They eat in a nearly ritu-
alistic manner, and want you to do so as well.
As Americans we feel we are often blundering
into a private party and haven't received all the
pertinent information. The following is some of
that information.

THE MENU A menu is a fixed-price meal, not that piece of paper
listing the food items. If you want what we consider a menu, you
need to ask for *la carte*. The menu is almost always posted on the
front of the restaurant so you know what you're getting into, both
foodwise and pricewise, before you enter. The fixed-price daily menu
(*menu fixe*) will generally include several choices for each of 2 or 3
courses. The daily fixed-price menu is cheaper than ordering off the
menu (*carte*). Our American term *à la carte* means 'of the menu,' in
case you hadn't noticed.

Restaurants frequently offer a plate of the day (*plat du
jour*), and some restaurants offer a set-price gourmet menu (*menu
dégustation*) of specialties of the chef. The price of a meal will occasionally include the house wine (*vin compris*).

A simple green salad (*salade verte*) is occasionally served
with or sometimes after the main course, before the cheese course or
dessert. Rarely is this type of salad even listed on the menu. Larger,
more involved–and to us what seem like full meals–salads such as
roquefort, *lardons* and *endive* are usually listed as first courses or
entrées. However, times have changed and you may now order a
green salad as an appetizer but you will most likely have to ask for it,
because, as we said earlier, you won't find it on the menu.

7

An *entrée* is a first course, the *plat* is the main course, followed by cheese and then dessert. Coffee is served at the end – never with your meal. There are all sorts of coffees that you can order decaffeinated which, if your meal is ending at midnight, as so often happens in Paris, you might want to consider. Ask for *déca* which rhymes with day-cah. You'll find a list of the different types of coffees on page 64.

WHY IS THERE A DOG AT THE TABLE NEXT TO ME? Parisians really love their dogs. It is not uncommon (no matter what type of eating establishment you are dining in) to find several dogs under tables, or even on their own chairs.

ASKING FOR YOUR BILL The bill in a restaurant is called *l'addition*...but the bill in a bar is called *le compte* or *la note*; confusing? It's easier if you just make a scribbling motion with your finger on the palm of your hand.

TIPPING A service charge is almost always added to your bill in Paris. Depending on the service, it is sometimes appropriate to leave an additional 5 to 10%. The menu will usually note that service is included (*service compris*). Sometimes this is abbreviated with the letters s.c. The letters s.n.c. stand for *service non compris*; this means that the service is not included in the price, and you must leave a tip.
You will sometimes find *couvert* or cover charge on your menu (a small charge just for placing your butt at the table).

MEALTIMES In Paris, lunch is served from noon to around 2:00 p.m., and dinner from 8:00 p.m. to 11:00 p.m. Restaurants usually have two seatings: at 8:00 or 8:30 p.m., and at 10:00 or 10:30 p.m. The restaurant will be less crowded at the early seating, but don't worry, it will fill up fast.

RESERVATIONS It's advisable if you're visiting a restaurant (as opposed to a *bistro* or *café*) to have reservations. Although you might see an empty restaurant and assume there will be seats available, most places we have listed will be full by 8:00 p.m. – with people who have made reservations. We advise making reservations in person. We like to do a walk-by in the afternoon, stop in and make reservations. Don't be afraid. The word for reservation is the same in English and French. You can do times and numbers with your fingers. If you speak a little French, you can do it on the phone. The problem with phoning, however, comes when, after you've said in a timid voice that you would like to make reservations if possible, they ask you a question in rapid-fire French and at that pace asking what your name is sounds pretty much like how many people are in the party or what time were you thinking about eating. Be patient; eventually you'll get the idea across.

WATER Europeans joke that you can tell a U.S. tourist from his "fanny pack," clothes and ubiquitous bottle of mineral water. Tap water is safe in Paris. Occasionally, you will find *non potable* signs in restrooms. This means that the water is not safe for drinking.

Waiters and waitresses often bring *eau minérale* (mineral water) to your table. You will be charged for it, so if you don't want mineral water ask for *une carafe d'eau* or *eau du robinet* (tap water).

WHAT TO DO WHEN NOTHING SEEMS TO BE OPEN Sundays can be frustrating. Nothing seems to be open. You can phone in advance but that isn't necessarily going to work because the place might not be open when you call. The best thing to do is to go to an area where there is a high concentration of restaurants. We have some of them listed on pages 14 and 15.

Fermé la Dimanche

Closed on Sunday.

We think of most of these places as restaurants. We have a hard time seeing the differences between many of these establishments. Cafés seem like bars, bistros seem like brasseries, and they all seem like restaurants. What some people think of as a limited-menu can seem complete to someone else (like us). Our full list of restaurants starting on page 18 includes cafés, brasseries, bistros and restaurants.

Alimentation: A small food store.

Auberge: An inn serving food and drink. These are most often found in the country, but restaurants in Paris also use the name.

Bar à café: Coffee shop serving light meals. Don't be misled by the name, though, as they rarely serve alcohol.

Bistro: Smaller and less fashionable than a restaurant, serving traditional, simple French food. Some are very similar to taverns or pubs.

Bar à champagne: Champagne bar.

Bar à vin: Wine bar.

Boucherie: Butcher's shop.

Boulangerie: Bakery. Nowhere else on earth can you get *baguettes* that taste like they do in France. Bread is often offered *bien cuit* (crusty) or *bien tendre* (doughy). Many *boulangeries* also sell sandwiches, tarts, quiches and small pizzas.

Brasserie: Originally, this term referred to a beer hall, but today serves food and drink.

Buffet: Eating establishment usually found in railroad stations.

Cabaret: Dinner and a show.

Café: Simple café dining is one of the pleasures of a trip to Paris. You can learn more sitting in a café for an hour than spending the day in a museum. In Paris, people-watching is like no other place in the world. Cafés serve alcoholic beverages and snacks. Some serve complete meals.

Cave: Cellar. This also refers to a wine shop. See Vins et Alcools.

Charcuteries: Originally these were pork butchers selling pork, ham, sausages, *jambon de Paris* and sometimes chicken. Now, most are delicatessens with prepared salads, quiches and other food tarts.

Chevaline: Horse-meat butcher's shop. These shops are becoming few and far between, but have a small and devoted clientele. Usually, there is a horse-head emblem on the front of the shop.

Chocolaterie: Chocolate shop.

Confiserie: Sweet shop.

Crémerie: Cream (and cheese) shop.

Crêperies: Popular for lunch, serving *crêpes* (thin filled pancakes).
Emporter: Carry-out foods.
Épicerie: Grocer's shop (literally "spice shop").
Express: Any establishment with this name is usually a snack bar.
Fromagerie: Serves up to 400 official types of cheese.
Glaces et Sorbets/Glacier: Ice cream and sorbet shop.

Berthillon
4th/Métro Pont-Marie
31 rue Saint-Louis-en-l'Ile (on the Île St-Louis)
Tel. 01/43.54.31.61
Closed Mon., Tue. and Aug.
Tourists and Parisians alike line up at the carry-out window for
the best-known ice cream in Paris. Over thirty flavors from *chocolat blanc* (white chocolate) to *pain d'épice* (gingerbread). It's on
one of the most beautiful streets in all of Paris.

Hostellerie: Upscale country restaurant.
Marché: Market.
Marchand de Légumes: Vegetable shop.
Pâtisseries: Pastry shops. The Parisian favorite of *baba au rhum*
(spongecake soaked in rum) was invented at **Stohrer**, 2nd/Métro Les
Halles, 51 rue Montorgueil, Closed part of Aug.
Pizzerias: You can figure this one out yourself.
Poissonnerie: Seafood shop.
Relais: Country inn or restaurant.
Restaurant: See our separate section on recommended restaurants.
Restoroute: Restaurant found on the highway.
Rôtisserie: Restaurant that usually specializes in roasted and grilled
meats, especially chicken.
Salon de Thé: Open mid-morning to late evening, serving light fare,
salads, cakes, ice cream and, of course, *thé* (tea).
Tabac: Bars where you can also buy cigarettes (they are, in fact, the
only places in France where you can buy tobacco), stamps, tickets for
public transportation, lottery tickets and phone cards. They are often
also *cafés*.
Traiteur: Delicatessen (this can also mean caterer). There seem to be
Indo-Chinese and Italian traiteurs all over the place. The food is usu-
ally good and inexpensive.
Triperie: Tripe shop.
Vins et Alcools: Wine and liquor shop.
Volailler: Poultry shop.

Even people who speak passable French can have trouble reading a menu. The grand-sounding *suprême de volaille* is simply a chicken breast. *Cervelle* is brains, but *cervelle de canut* is an herbed cheese spread from Lyon.

Remember that the dish that you ordered may not be exactly as described in this guide. Every chef is (and should be) innovative. What we have listed for you in this guide is the most common version of a dish. Be careful, menus in English are often wrong.

Times can change and restaurants can close, so do a walk-by earlier in the day or the day before, if possible.

Each of our recommended restaurants offers something different. Some have great food and little ambiance. Others have great ambiance and adequate food. Still others have both. Our goal is to find restaurants that are moderately priced and enjoyable. All restaurants have been tried and tested. Not enough can be said for a friendly welcome and great service. No matter how fabulous the food is, your dining experience will always be better when you're treated well.

 ## Tips for Budget Dining in Paris

There is no need to spend a lot of money in Paris to have good food. Of course it helps when the euro is weaker than the dollar, but there are all kinds of fabulous foods to be had inexpensively all over Paris.

Eat at a neighborhood restaurant or bistro. You'll always know the price of a meal before entering, as almost all Paris restaurants post the menu and prices in the window. Never order anything whose price is not known in advance. If you see *selon grosseur* (sometimes abbreviated as s/g) this means that you are paying by weight, which can be extremely expensive.

Restaurants and bistros that have menus written in English (especially those near tourist attractions) are almost always more expensive than neighborhood restaurants and bistros.

Delis, *traiteurs* and food stores can provide cheap and wonderful meals. Buy some cheese, bread, wine and other snacks and have a picnic in one of Paris's great parks. In fact, no matter what, you should go into a *boulangerie* and buy a *baguette* at least once. Remember to pack a corkscrew and eating utensils when you leave home.

Lunch, even at the most expensive restaurants listed in this guide, always has a lower fixed price. So, have lunch as your main meal.

Large department stores frequently have supermarkets in the basement and restaurants that have reasonably priced food and wine. The ultimate grocery store (with wine cellar and carry-out) is **La Grande Épicerie** located in Au Bon Marché department store (7th/Métro Sèvres-Babylone, 38 rue de Sèvres, closed Sun.). Don't miss it! It's also interesting to visit the supermarkets in **Monoprix**, the discount department store chain. Not at all like at home.

Street vendors generally sell inexpensive and terrific food; you'll find excellent hot dogs, *crêpes* and roast-chicken sandwiches all over Paris. At lunch time, you'll see Parisians eating long, thin *baguettes* filled with chicken, mayonnaise and sliced eggs throughout the city. And, for the cost of a cup of coffee or a drink, you can linger at a café and watch the world pass you by for as long as you want. It's one of Paris's greatest bargains.

Kids love **Hippopotamus**, a chain of inexpensive restaurants with many locations in Paris. They have noisy televisions everywhere, paper table covers for coloring (they provide crayons), and balloons (everything you thought you'd left behind at home).

And don't eat at McDonald's, for God's sake.

If nothing else, food markets are very interesting. Though you may feel intimidated by the wild goings-on (not to mention the sights and smells) it is absolutely worth a trip to see a real outdoor Parisian market. Filled with colorful vendors, stinky cheese, fresh produce, poultry and hanging rabbits, this is real Paris at its most diverse and beautiful. Parisians still shop (some every day) at food markets around the city. Unless noted otherwise, all are open Tuesday through noon on Sunday. Some of the best-known are:

Rue Montorgueil, 1st/Métro Les Halles
Rue Mouffetard, 5th/Métro Censier-Daubenton
Rue de Buci, 6th/Métro Mabillon
Marché Raspail, 6th/Métro Rennes (open Sunday) (organic)
Rue Cler, 7th/Métro École Militaire
Marché Bastille on the boulevard Richard Lenoir,
    11th/Métro Bastille (open Thursday and Sunday)
Rue Daguerre, 14th/Métro Denfert-Rochereau
Rue Poncelet, 17th/Métro Ternes

Markets are places that you might appreciate as you would a museum, but there are other places around Paris where you can also see and experience food in a unique setting. The area around the Place de la Madeleine (8th/  Métro Madeleine) is packed with fabulous specialty food shops (the windows of the food store **Fauchon** are worth a trip by themselves), wine dealers, restaurants, and tea rooms. This is a perfect place for eating and purchasing culinary souvenirs. There is something for every taste – but this is an upscale area, and can be expensive.

In addition to food markets and specialty shops, there are several areas in Paris where many restaurants are concentrated in small pockets. These are areas that are charming just in and of themselves, nice to walk through and nice to eat in, particularly outside on a nice evening.

One area is on **rue Pot-de-Fer** between la rue Tournefort and la rue Mouffetard, just off the market. It's a slip of a street but it's lined with charming restaurants with clothed tables set for dinner, colored lights hanging from the roof overhangs, and a uniquely Parisian ambiance (Métro Monge).

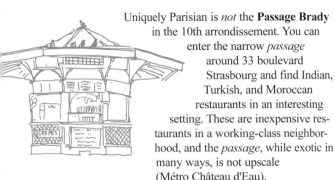

Uniquely Parisian is *not* the **Passage Brady** in the 10th arrondissement. You can enter the narrow *passage* around 33 boulevard Strasbourg and find Indian, Turkish, and Moroccan restaurants in an interesting setting. These are inexpensive restaurants in a working-class neighborhood, and the *passage*, while exotic in many ways, is not upscale (Métro Château d'Eau).

There are several restaurants and bars on the lovely **Place Sainte-Catherine** (enter from rue Caron off of rue St-Antoine) in the Marais. The Place Sainte-Catherine is a special, quiet respite in this fashionable area (Métro St-Paul).

You'll find loads of restaurants **off of la rue Saint-Jacques** in the area around la rue Saint-Séverin and la rue de la Huchette in the 5th. This area, a short walk from Notre Dame, is filled with French, Italian, Greek and other restaurants jammed into small streets. It's a very pleasant walk, and you're bound to find somewhere to eat. Nearby in the 6th is the **cour du Commerce**, a tiny alleyway off of la rue St-André-des-Arts, which is lined with restaurants to fit all pocketbooks (Métros Saint-Michel, Odéon or Cluny-La Sorbonne).

TEN SIMPLE RULES
OF DINING IN PARIS

1. Just because you're a tourist, you don't have to eat like one. Looking for a place to eat while sightseeing? Here's a hint: If the menu is posted in English, there's a good chance the restaurant caters to tourists…which means that you'll probably not only be overcharged, you'll miss out on experiencing an authentic French dining experience. This guide will help you discover where the locals eat.

2. Don't be afraid. They can't and won't hurt you. They are not laughing at you, they don't dislike you, they aren't even thinking about you. Waiters in France are trained professionals whose job is to serve you. Despite what you've heard, they want you to have a good time. Sometimes they are just mystified by what we do.

When asked what the French think about Thanksgiving Julia Child replied "The French aren't thinking about Thanksgiving, they're focused on themselves. Which pretty much sums it up.

3. Don't ever call the waiter "*garçon.*" Though sometimes in bars a Parisian will use this word, travelers should never use it.

4. Try to make reservations. This isn't as difficult as it seems; the words are similar in both languages and they'll get the gist of what you're trying to do. We often do a walk-by in the afternoon and stop in to make the reservation. When we go back that night they are almost always happy to see us again.

5. Return to a restaurant if you like it. If you have the luxury of time and can withstand the temptation to try other restaurants, you will always be treated better if they recognize you. Few travelers return to the same restaurant.

6. Parisians dine leisurely. Don't expect to get the same speed of service as at home. For the French, dinner is nearly a ritual. In its full-blown form, it begins with an *apéritif*. This is often accompanied

by an *amuse-gueule*, a little snack of some sort. After this, you order an *hors-d'oeuvre*. Then comes an *entrée*, which is a first course – *pâté* or a composed salad, such as a salad with shrimp or hard-boiled eggs – and then the main course which will most likely be meat or fish. The main course is sometimes accompanied by or followed by a salad, but it is a simple green salad. After this, just when you think you're going to explode and have secretly unbuckled your belt, the *serveur* arrives with selections from the cheese platter that are followed by dessert, and, finally, coffee. But if you do not want to follow the French protocol, don't. Even if the waiter seems to disapprove, do what you like.

7. Don't talk loudly. You will notice that the French speak softly, Americans don't; we just can't help it. But believe us: Those loud voices coupled with running shoes, backpacks, "fanny packs," large, conspicuous guide books and cameras are like wearing a neon sign announcing that you are a tourist, an American tourist.

8. Stand your ground without being aggressive. In the years we've been traveling, it seems that waiters have become more relaxed about the rituals of eating, and will accommodate you if you insist on what you want – within reason, of course.

9. Visit a street vendor at least once in Paris. Whether it's sandwiches, hot dogs or *crêpes*, Parisian street vendors sell delicious "food on the run." Do yourself a favor, and sample some.

10. Always be courteous. Remember that you are a guest in their country. There are simple things that the French do that we don't, like excusing yourself or saying please all the time.

S'il vous plaît (seel voo play) after nearly everything is a safe way to be very polite. Seriously. A polite Parisian ALWAYS finishes a greeting (such as *bonjour* – hello) or affirmation (such as *oui* – yes) with a title. Thus, *bonjour* is always *bonjour, madame* or *m'sieur* and yes or no is always *oui, m'sieur* or *madame*. And just so you know, you say *bonjour*, which is essentially hello, all day and night. *Bonsoir* – good evening – is reserved for leaving and after 7:00 p.m., and *bonne nuit* – good night – is only used when you are actually on your way to bed.

❧ Places To Eat ❧

Phone numbers, days closed and hours of operation often change, so it's advisable to check ahead. Restaurants in tourist areas may have different hours and days of operation

Oui m'sieur? Combien de personnes?

during low season. Reservations are recommended for all restaurants unless noted. The telephone country code for France is 33. When calling within France you must dial the area code. The area code for Paris is 01. However, you do not use the 0 before the area code when calling France from the U.S. or Canada. Confused?

Here's what it looks like:

From the United States:
(011) 33 1/43.26.48.23

From within Paris:
01/43.26.48.23

Prices are for a main course and without wine.
Lunch, even at the most expensive restaurants listed below, always has a lower fixed price. Credit cards accepted unless noted.

Inexpensive: under 10 euros
Moderate: 11 - 20 euros
Expensive: 21 - 30 euros
Very Expensive: over 30 euros

Albion *Map p. 124 #1*

This wine shop/bistro, located in the gentrifying 10th,
not far from Gare du Nord and Gare de l'Est, is run by
English chef Matthew Ong and New Zealand *sommelière* Hayden
Clout. You'll find dark plank floors and walls lined with wine bot-
tles. Servers are efficient (and if you don't speak French, you'll be
just fine). Inventive, limited, menu and interesting wine list.
Worth the trip. *Info*: 10th/Métro Poissonière. 80 rue du Faubourg
Poissonière (at rue des Messageries). Tel. 01/42.46.02.44. Closed
Sun. and Mon. www.restaurantalbion.com. Moderate.

L'Ange 20 *Map p. 124 #2*

Don't miss this small, intimate restaurant in the heart of the Marais
near the Centre Pompidou. Friendly, efficient, and attentive service. You can watch the chef in the open kitchen. Lively mix of
tourists and Parisians enjoying reasonably priced meals. Try the
excellent *agneau façon sept heures* (lamb cooked for seven hours).
Unbelievable what the chef turns out in this small kitchen. *Info*: 4th/
Métro Rambuteau. 8 rue Geoffroy L'Angevin (off of rue Beaubourg).
Tel. 01/40.27.93.67. No lunch. Closed Mon. www.lange20.com
Moderate.

L'Avant Goût *Map p. 125 #1*

Mix with the French in this small, crowded bistro near the place
d'Italie. Consistently good cuisine and very French. Try the *pot-au-
feu* (stew of meat and vegetables). *Info*: 13th/Métro Place d'Italie. 26
rue Bobillot (from place d'Italie, south on rue Bobillot).
Tel. 01/53.80.24.00. Closed Sun., Mon. and most of Aug.
www.lavantgout.com. Moderate.

Au Bascou *Map p. 124 #3*

This tiny bistro serves Basque specialties such as *piperade* (a spicy
omelet). It doesn't look like much from the outside, but the food will
not disappoint. Try the delicious *épaule d'agneau* (lamb shoulder)
or *cabillaud poêlé* (fried cod). Interesting regional wine list. Too bad
they're closed on weekends. *Info*: 3rd/Métro Arts-et-Métiers. 38 rue
Réaumur (at rue Volta). Tel. 01/42.72.69.25. Closed Sat., Sun. and
part of Aug. www.au-bascou.fr. Moderate.

Bistro des Deux Théâtres *Map p. 124 #4*

Affordable dining at this neighborhood bistro near the place de Clichy. Excellent *foie gras de canard* (fattened duck liver). *Info*: 9th/ Métro Trinité. 18 rue Blanche (at rue Moncey). Tel. 01/45.26.41.43 Open daily. www.bistrocie.fr. Moderate.

Bistrot de L'Oulette *Map p. 127 #1*

Intimate bistro in the Marais (near the place des Vosges) featuring the specialties of Southwest France (especially *confit de canard*). *Info*: 4th/Métro Bastille. 38 rue des Tournelles (near rue du Pas-de-la-Mule). Tel. 01/42.71.43.33. Closed Sat. (lunch) and Sun. www.l-oulette.com. Moderate.

Bistrot Paul-Bert *Map p. 127 #2*

A truly neighborhood bistro experience from its traditional decor to its menu written on a blackboard. Extensive wine list. Try the *entrecôte* (rib-eye steak) and the delicious *soufflé au chocolat*. *Info*: 11th/Métro Faidherbe-Chaligny. 18 rue Paul-Bert (near rue Chanzy). Tel. 01/43.72.24.01. Closed Sun., Mon. and Aug. Moderate.

For inventive small plates, head down the street to **Le 6 Paul-Bert**. 6 rue Paul-Bert. Tel. 01/43.79.14.32. Closed Sun. and Mon. Moderate.

Bistrotters

You won't mind the trek to this out-of-the-way neighborhood restaurant, where you'll find friendly, English-speaking *A bit out of the way but worth the tr[...]* servers. Start with the *salsa de guacamole, tempura de gambas* (king prawn with guacamole salsa). For a main course, try the excellent *croustillant de poitrine de cochon au fenouil* (crispy pork belly with fennel). For dessert, order the *pan perdu de brioche, caramel au beurre salé* (brioche bread pudding with salted-butter caramel sauce). A great experience for 30 euros for two courses. Note that reservations are made 12 days in advance through their website, and must be reconfirmed by email 48 hours before. It's worth the effort. *Info*: 14th/Métro Plaisance. 9 rue Decrés. Tel. 01.45.45.58.59. Closed Sun. and Mon. www.bistrotters.com. *From métro take rue d'Alésia, turn right on rue Decrés (one minute, .1 miles).* Moderate.

La Boulangerie *Map p. 127 #3*

Classic French bistro with a mosaic floor in a former bakery near Père-Lachaise cemetery. Highlights include *rognon de veau* (veal kidneys), *caille* (quail), and *cabillaud* (cod) served with risotto. Good selection of wines by the glass. *Info*: 20th/Métro Ménilmontant. 15 rue des Panoyaux (off of blvd. de Ménilmontant). Tel. 01/43.58.45.45. Closed Sat. (lunch), Sun. and Mon. (lunch). www.laboulangerie-bistrot.fr. Moderate.

Chardenoux *Map p. 127 #4*

This small, beautiful bistro has been in business for almost 100 years. Cyril Lignac, of television cooking-show fame, has taken over and updated its menu (and prices). The weekday *prix fixe* lunch at less than 30 euros lets you sample such dishes as *penne aux coquillages et chipirons, crème basilic* (penne w/shellfish and squid in a basil cream sauce). *Info*: 11th/Métro Charonne. 1 rue Jules-Vallès and 23 rue Chanzy. Tel. 01/43.71.49.52. Open daily. www.restaurantlechardenoux.com. Moderate - Expensive.

Chez Janou *Map p. 127 #5*

Everyone seems to be having a great time at this bistro, a few blocks from the place des Vosges. Provençal and straightforward French food (very good *entrecôte*). Decent-priced wines with an emphasis on those from Provence. Known for its selection of *pastis* (anise-flavored aperitif) and delicious bowl of *mousse au chocolat* (chocolate mousse). Not the greatest food in Paris, but certainly lots of fun. *Info*: 3rd/Métro Chemin Vert. 2 rue Roger-Verlomme (at rue des Tournelles). Tel. 01/42.72.28.41. Open daily. www.chezjanou.com. Moderate.

Chez Paul *Map p. 127 #6*

A favorite bistro in Paris. Never a bad meal, and ask to eat upstairs. Try *rillettes de lapin au romarin* (rabbit seasoned with rosemary), *os à moelle* (marrow bone), and the deliciously creamy *gratin dauphinois* (potatoes with eggs, cream, and cheese). *Info*: 11th/Métro Bastille or Ledru-Rollin. 13 rue de Charonne (at rue de Lappe). Tel. 01/47.00.34.57. Open daily. www.chezpaul.com. Moderate.

La Fontaine de Mars *Map p. 124 #5*

Red-checked tablecloths and friendly *One of our all-time favorites!*
service near the Eiffel Tower. Try the
poulet fermier aux morilles (free-range
chicken with morel mushrooms). Prices seem to have increased
since the Obamas ate here. Still, highly recommended. *Info*: 7th/
Métro Ecole-Militaire. 129 rue St-Dominique (near Avenue
Bosquet). Tel. 01/47.05.46.44. Open daily.
www.fontainedemars.com. Moderate.

Frenchie Bar à Vins *Map p. 124 #6*

You can sample Chef Gregory Marchand's dishes at this wine-bar
annex to his (famously difficult to get into) bistro Frenchie. The
menu consists of small plates. Try *terrine de campagne* and down it
with a glass of wine from the interesting wine list. To score a table,
you must arrive before 7:00 p.m. *Info*: 2nd/Métro Sentier. 6 rue du
Nil (between rue d'Aboukir and rue Réaumur). No telephone. No
reservations. No lunch. Closed Sat. and Sun. Moderate. **Restaurant
Frenchie** is at 5 rue du Nil, Tel. 01/40.39.96.19 (reservations).
Closed Sat. and Sun. www.frenchie-restaurant.com. Expensive.

Down the street at 9 rue du Nil is **Frenchie To Go** featuring fish and
chips, pickles, smoked bacon, and a delicious reuben sandwich. No
reservations. There are 15 seats if you want to eat on the premises,
and you can wash down your food with ginger beer. Open Mon.
to Fri. 8:30 a.m. to 4:30 p.m., Sat. and Sun. 9:30 a.m. to 5:30 p.m.
Breakfast served all day. www.frenchietogo.com.
Inexpensive-Moderate.

Le Fumoir *Map p. 124 #7*

This bar and restaurant is located near the Louvre. It's known for its
Sunday brunch, salads, happy hour and *gâteau chocolat* (chocolate
cake). There's a library in the back where you can have a drink and
read (and exchange your own books for the ones in their library).
Info: 1st/Métro Louvre-Rivoli. 6 rue de l'Amiral-de Coligny
(between rue de Rivoli and the River Seine). Tel. 01/42.92.00.24.
Open daily 11 a.m. to 2 a.m. Closed part of Aug.
www.lefumoir.com. Inexpensive - Moderate.

Gaspard de la Nuit *Map p. 127 #7*

This cozy restaurant is located in the Marais between the place de la Bastille and place des Vosges. Traditional French cuisine. Try the delicious *carré d'agneau en croûte d'herbs* (loin of lamb with herbs) or the *coquilles Saint-Jacques* (scallops) served with *chou-fleur* (cauliflower). Always an enjoyable experience. *Info*: 4th/Métro Bastille. 6 rue des Tournelles (near rue du Pas-de-la-Mule). Tel. 01/42.77.90.53. Open daily. No lunch. www.legaspard.fr. Moderate - Expensive.

Le Grand 8 *Map p. 126 #2*

This friendly, small bistro is located in Montmartre near Sacrè-Coeur. Unlike most places in this touristy area, most diners are from the neighborhood. Start with a *salade de chèvre chaud* (warm goat cheese salad) and dine on such main courses as *carré d'agneau accompagné d'un gratin de pommes de terre* (rack of lamb with potato *gratin*). Interesting selection of wines by the glass and bottle. Ask for a seat near the back window and enjoy the great view. *Info*: 18th/Métro Anvers or Lamarck-Caulaincourt. 8 rue Lamarck. Tel. 01/42.55.04.55. Closed Mon. and Tues. No lunch except Sat. and Sun. www.legrand8.fr. Moderate.

Le Hangar *Map p. 124 #8*

Nothing fancy about this bistro near the Pompidou Center. Classic French food at reasonable prices. The menu features *soupe au potiron* (pumpkin soup), *lapereau* (rabbit), and pan-fried *foie gras*. Excellent *gâteau au chocolat* (chocolate cake). *Info*: 3rd/Métro Rambuteau. 12 impasse Berthaud (off of rue Beaubourg). Tel. 01/42.74.55.44. Closed Sun., Mon. and Aug. No credit cards. Inexpensive - Moderate.

Je Thé ... Me *Map p. 125 #2*

This attractive bistro in a century-old grocery store serves classic French fare. Start with the *foie gras de canard* (fattened duck liver). For your main course, order the *carré d'agneau rôti au thym* (roasted rack of lamb with thyme) or the *coquilles Saint-Jacques* (scallops) in a citrus sauce. Friendly service. *Info*: 15th/Métro Vaugirard. 4 rue d'Alleray (off of rue de Vaugirard). Tel. 01/48.42.48.30. Closed Sun., Mon. and Aug. Moderate.

The name is a play on Je t'aime... I Love you.

Juvenile's *Map p. 124 #9*

This inexpensive, unpretentious wine bar serves light meals and has a large, interesting New- and Old-World wine selection. Friendly and fun. Order traditional wine-bar fare or, if you're tired of French food, try the haggis. (The owner, originally from Scotland, has just turned over the place to his daughter.) Have the *terrine de campagne* (pork and liver *pâté*) when available. *Info*: 1st/ Métro Bourse. 47 rue de Richelieu (near rue des Petits Champs). Tel. 01/42.97.46.49. Closed Sun and Mon (lunch). Inexpensive-Moderate.

La Laiterie Sainte-Clotilde *Map p. 124 #10*

The blackboard menu features French comfort food. You'll dine (in a former milk and cheese shop) with a chic local crowd. A down-to-earth bistro in an expensive neighborhood (not too far from the Musée d'Orsay). Try the *oeufs meurette* (poached eggs in red wine sauce) or the tasty *blanquette de veau* (veal stew). *Info*: 7th/ Métro Solférino or Rue du Bac. 64 rue de Bellechasse (off of rue de Grenelle). Tel. 01/45.51.74.61. Closed Sun. Moderate.

Oudino *Map p. 125 #3*

This bistro is located on an attractive small street. You can start your meal with a *salade caesar* (Caesar salad) and dine on excellent *entrecôte* served with a *béarnaise* sauce. A real find. *Info*: 7th/ Métro Vaneau. 17 rue Oudinot (off of blvd. des Invalides). Tel. 01/45.66.05.09. Closed Sat. (lunch) and Sun. www.oudino.fr. Moderate.

Osteria Ruggera *Map p. 124 #11*

This intimate restaurant in the increasingly hip, pedestrian Montorgueil area serves delicious Italian dishes. Try the *dégustation de 5 entrées pour 2 personnes* (five antipasti for two persons) and wash it down with a bottle of Primitivo. Excellent *gnocchi de pommes de terre avec noix et gorgonzola* (potato gnocchi with gorgonzola and walnuts). *Info*: 2nd/Métro Etienne Marcel. 35 rue Tiquetonne (off of rue Montorgueil). Tel. 01/40.26.13.91. Closed Sun. (lunch). www.osteria-ruggera.fr. Moderate. The casual sister restaurant **O'scià** is located across the street and serves decent pizza.

Les Papilles *Map p. 125 #4*

Near the Panthéon, *Les Papilles* (Tastebuds) sells gourmet foods and wine, and offers creative takes on French cuisine. Try the tender hanger steak. Especially interesting is the *thon roti aux 4 épices et sesame grille* (tuna roasted with four spices and grilled sesame). Worth the trip! *Info*: 5th/Métro Cluny-La Sorbonne (RER Luxembourg). 30 rue Gay-Lussac (near rue Saint-Jacques). Tel. 01/43.25.20.79. Closed Sun., Mon. and part of Aug. www.lespapillesparis.fr. Moderate.

Le Petit Bal Perdu *Map p. 127 #8*

You'll enjoy the relaxed vibe at this friendly and youthful bar/restaurant in the increasingly trendy Oberkampf neighborhood. Start with the *salade aux figues et poires* (fig and pear salad). For a main course, have the *parmentier de canard aux cèpes* (duck with mushrooms and potatoes), the *entrecôte avec pommes de terre* (rib-eye steak with potatoes), or the delicious burger gorganzola (hamburger with blue cheese). The *mousse légère a la chataîgne et sa glace au nougat* (chestnut mousse with nougat ice-cream) is a great way to end your meal. *Info*: 11th/Métro Oberkampf. 25 rue Oberkampf (off of blvd. Voltaire). Tel. 01/48.06.28.23. Closed Sat. (lunch) and Sun. Moderate.

Le Petit Marché *Map p. 127 #9*

This corner café/restaurant, located on a small street off the place des Vosges, is not for those who want a quiet, romantic dinner. It's busy, noisy, and jam-packed (don't come here if you don't like to be seated in cramped quarters). The staff is helpful and friendly and most speak English. Start with the Chinese salad (*salade chinois*) or the *ceviche*. You'll find French cuisine with Asian influences such as fresh tuna tartar (*thon cru*) with toasted sesame seeds served with a Thai sauce. Main courses are served with small bowls of mashed potatoes and green beans (*haricot verts*). Other recommended dishes include the cod (*cabillaud*), lamb (*agneau*), *steak tartare* with Asian spices, and the succulent duck breast (*magret de canard*) in a honey sauce. Try the excellent raspberry (*framboise*) dessert. *Info*: 3rd/Métro Chemin Vert. 9 rue Béarn (at rue des Minimes). Tel. 01/42.72.06.67. Open daily. Moderate.

Another favorite.

Au Petit Marguery *Map p. 125 #5*

This 1930s bistro features outstanding game dishes and is known for its Grand Marnier *soufflé* and good service. Try the interesting *pavé d'espadon, écrasée de pommes de terre au basilic et sauce Riviera* (swordfish wtih basil mash potatoes and "Riviera" sauce of olive oil, basil, cucumber, tomatoes and anchovy). Good old-fashioned French cuisine. *Info*: 13th/Métro Les Gobelins. 9 boulevard de Port-Royal (near av. des Gobelins). Tel. 01/43.31.58.59. Open daily. www.petit-marguery.fr. Moderate.

Le Petit Prince de Paris *Map p. 125 #6*

Walk through the velvet curtains and enter the intimate dining room at this funky, fun, and friendly bistro near the Sorbonne. There are several *prix-fixe* (fixed-priced) menus. Try the *magret de canard* (breast of fattened duck). Vegetarians will enjoy the *plat végétarien* (a delicious assortment of warm and cold vegetables). Fantastic chocolate desserts. *Info*: 5th/Métro Maubert-Mutualité. 12 rue de Lanneau (near rue des Ecoles). Tel. 01/43.54.77.26. Open daily for dinner. www.lepetitprincedeparis.fr. Moderate.

Au Petit Riche *Map p. 124 #12*

This classic bistro, with authentic 1880s decor, serves specialties of the Loire Valley with a Parisian twist. Try the *vol-au vent de ris de veau* (puff pastry filled with veal sweetbreads). Very popular with tourists. *Info*: 9th/Métro Le Peletier or Richelieu-Drouot. 25 rue Le Peletier (at rue Rossini). Tel. 01/47.70.68.68. Open daily. www.restaurant-aupetitriche.com. Moderate.

Le Potager du Père Thierry *Map p. 126 #4*

You'll receive a warm welcome at this tiny, noisy 26-seat restaurant on a touristy street in Montmartre, where you'll feel you stumbled into a fun party. Start with the excellent *oeufs en cocotte foie gras* (duck foie gras mixed with an egg). For a main course, try the *coquilles* (scallops) or the duck *confit* with mashed potatoes. For dessert, don't miss the tasty white chocolate *mousse* with raspberries. This is good rustic food, and you won't be disappointed. *Info*: 18th/Métro Anvers. 16 rue des Trois Frères. Tel. 01/53.28.26.20. Open daily. No lunch. Moderate.

Quedubon
Join the neighborhood locals at this wine bar, wine shop, and bistro
located near the Parc des Buttes-Chaumont. You'll choose from a list
of inexpensive, organic wines from the ever-changing chalkboard.
Loved the farm chicken with braised endive. Excellent and large
platter of *charcuterie*. *Info*: 19th/Métro Buttes Chaumont. 22 Rue du
Plateau (off of rue Botzaris). Tel. 01/85.08.54.68. Close Sat. (lunch),
Sun., and Mon. www.restaurantquedubon.fr. Moderate.

Le Richer *Map p. 124 #13*
This attractive café, bar, and restaurant with exposed stone walls
serves breakfast, lunch, and dinner. Try the tender *suprême de
volaille* (chicken breast) or the Japanese-inspired *tartare de bœuf,
huîtres, granny smith, radis et sesame* (raw beef with oysters, Granny
Smith apples, radishes and sesame). Pleasant service. *Info*: 9th/Métro
Poissonnière or Bonne Nouvelle. 2 rue Richer (near rue du Faubourg
Poissonnière). No reservations. Open daily. www.facebook.com/
Restaurant.Le.Richer. Moderate.

Le Reminet *Map p. 125 #7*
This quaint bistro is located in the Latin Quarter near St-Michel and
just across the river from Notre-Dame. Helpful staff and the romantic
atmosphere (down to candelabras on the tables) make for a wonderful evening. Start with a *kir royal* (an aperitif made with champagne
and *creme de cassis*). Try the *piccatta de veau* (veal piccatta) or
pot-au-feu (a stew of meat and vegetables). Good wine list featuring
wines from all French regions. *Info*: 5th/Métro Maubert-Mutualité or
St-Michel. 5 rue des Grands-Degrés (one block south of Quai de la
Tournelle at rue Mâitre-Albert). Tel. 01/44.07.04.24. Open daily.
www.lereminet.com. Moderate - Expensive.

Restaurant de la Tour *Map p. 125 #8*
You'll be welcomed by the friendly owners to the lovely dining
room with Provençal décor where you'll dine on classic French
fare. Try the delicious *sanglier* (wild boar) or the *ris de veau aux
morilles* (veal sweetbreads with morel mushrooms). After dinner, head to the brilliantly lit Eiffel Tower, just a few blocks away.
Info: 15th/Métro Dupleix. 6 rue Desaix (near av. de Suffren). Tel.
01/43.06.04.24. Closed Sat., Sun., and Aug.
www.restaurant-delatour.fr. Moderate - Expensive.

Sorza *Map p. 125 #9*

This small, modern Italian restaurant with stark red-and-black decor is located on the lovely Île St-Louis. Try the *filet de volaille aux morilles et fetuccine* (chicken fillet with morels and fetuccine) and end with the sinfully rich *mousse au chocolat* (chocolate mousse). *Info*: 4th/Métro Pont-Marie. 51 rue Saint-Louis-en-I'lle (on the Île St-Louis). Tel. 01/43.54.78.62. Open daily. www.sorza.fr. Moderate.

Le Souk *Map p. 127 #10*

This popular Moroccan restaurant with a good selection of vegetarian dishes is always busy and the interior is exotic. Try a delicious *tajine* (Moroccan stew of meat or poultry and vegetables flavored with spices). *Info*: 11th/Métro Bastille or Ledru-Rollin. 1 rue Keller (near rue Charonne). Tel. 01/49.29.05.08. Closed Mon. www.le-souk-paris. com. Moderate.

Spring *Map p. 124 #14*

Who would have thought that a Chicago-born chef would be creating the biggest buzz in Paris dining? Daniel Rose has moved from his tiny restaurant into a modern, sleek space near the Louvre. Reserve well in advance. The menu changes daily and you'll be served what everyone else is having. A delicious experience that you won't soon forget. Interesting wine list. *Info*: 1st/Métro Louvre-Rivoli. 6 rue Bailleul (one block north of rue de Rivoli, off of rue du Louvre). Tel. 01/45.96.05.72. Open dinner Tue.to Sat. Reservations required. www.springparis.fr. Very Expensive.

Le Taxi Jaune *Map p. 124 #15*

You'll find the intimate "Yellow Taxi" on a backstreet in the Marais. The menu changes regularly and although it often includes offal and horse (*cheval*), there are plenty of other choices. Service is friendly, unobtrusive, and unhurried. Try the pumpkin and vegetable soup when available. If you're looking for a relaxing dining experience in the Marais, you've found the place. *Info*: 3rd/Métro Arts-et-Méiters. 13 rue Chapon (between rue du Temple and rue Beaubourg). Tel. 01/42.76.00.40. Closed Sat. and Sun. www.restaurantletaxijaune.fr. Moderate.

These restaurants are very expensive and highly praised. Reservations well in advance are a must, as are jacket and tie.

Alain Ducasse *Map p.124 A*
Restaurant Plaza Athénée
8th/Métro Alma-Marceau
25 avenue Montaigne
Tel. 01/53.67.65.00
www.alain-ducasse.com

L'Ambroisie *Map p.125 A*
4th/Métro St-Paul
9 place des Vosges
Tel. 01/42.78.51.45
www.ambroisie-paris.com

L'Arpège *Map p.125 B*
7th/Métro Varenne
84 rue de Varenne
Tel. 01/47.05.09.06
www.alain-passard.com

L'Atelier de Joël Robuchon
Map p.125 C
7th/Métro Rue du Bac
5 rue de Montalembert
Tel. 01/42.22.56.56
www.joel-robuchon.net

Le Cinq *Map p.124 B*
8th/Métro George V
31 avenue George V (in the Four Seasons George V)
Tel. 01/49.52.71.54
www.restaurant-lecinq.com

Epicure (Le Bristol) *Map p.124 C*
8th/Métro Miromesnil
112 rue du Faubourg St-Honoré
Tel. 01/53.43.43.40
www.lebristolparis.com

Le Grand Véfour *Map p.124 D*
1st/Métro Palais-Royal
17 rue de Beaujolais
Tel. 01/42.96.56.27
www.grand-vefour.com

Guy Savoy *Map p.124 E*
17th/Métro Charles-de-Gaulle-
Étoile or Ternes
18 rue Troyon
Tel. 01/43.80.40.61
www.guysavoy.com

Jules Verne *Map p.124 F*
7th/Métro Bir-Hakeim
Second level of the Eiffel Tower
Tel. 01/45.55.61.44
www.alain-ducasse.com

Lucas Carton *Map p.124 G*
8th/Métro Madeleine
9 place de la Madeleine
Tel. 01/42.65.22.90
www.lucascarton.com

Pierre Gagnaire *Map p.124 H*
8th/Métro George V
6 rue Balzac (Hôtel Balzac)
Tel. 01/58.36.12.50
www.pierre-gagnaire.com

Taillevent *Map p.124 I*
8th/Métro George V
15 rue Lamennais
Tel. 01/44.95.15.01
www.taillevent.com

La Tour d'Argent *Map p.125 D*
5th/Métro Maubert-Mutualité
15-17 quai de la Tournelle
Tel. 01/43.54.23.31
www.latourdargent.com

Le Timbre *Map p. 125 #10*

The name means "stamp," which is appropriate for this tiny Left Bank bistro. It's a wonderful Parisian experience. In fall 2014, chef Charles Danet and his wife Agnès Peyre took over this long-time favorite. Three fixed-priced menus are offered (34/41/49 euro). The first is a three-course meal with a main course featuring meat. The second adds a fish course (try the *dorade* [sea bream] served with sautéed leeks), and the third adds *foie gras*. The menu changes daily. End your meal with homemade ice cream. *Info*: 6th/Métro Notre-Dame-des-Champs. 3 rue Sainte-Beuve (off of rue Notre-Dame-des-Champs). Closed Sun., Mon. and part of Aug. Tel. 01/45.49.10.40. www.restaurantletimbre.com. Moderate - Expensive.

La Veraison *Map p. 125 #11*

This casual restaurant is a real find. You'll see the chef cooking as you walk in. The food is a modern take on traditional French cooking. And it's fun to go off the beaten path. Chef Ulla Bosse serves innovative dishes such as *raviole de foie gras* (*foie gras* ravioli). Don't miss her risotto and the *quenelles de chocolat noir à la glace caramel beurre salé* (chocolate dessert with salted caramel ice cream). *Info*: 15th/Métro Commerce. 64 rue de la Croix Nivert (at rue du Théâtre). Tel. 01/45.32.39.39. Closed Sun. and Mon. No lunch. www.laveraison.com. Moderate.

Verjus Bar à Vins *Map p. 124 #16*

A French wine bar with an American twist. Braden Perkins, an American chef and owner of the restaurant Verjus, opened this popular eatery. Small plates (there are usually three choices) and an excellent wine selection from Laura Adrian, the sommelier. Try the delicious fried chicken sandwich! No reservations. *Info*: 1st/Métro Bourse, Pyramides or Palais-Royal. 47 rue de Montpensier. Tel. 01/42.97.54.40. Dinner Mon-Fri. Closed Sat and Sun. www.verjusparis.com. Inexpensive - Moderate.

Vivant Table *Map p. 124 #17*

Swiss-born Pierre Jancou has opened this casual wine bar/bistro in a colorfully tiled small shop that once sold exotic birds. You'll find Italian-Franco home-cooking in a funky neighborhood. Try the grilled *poularde* with organic vegetables. Excellent *foie gras* with *bortsch de betteraves* (beet soup). Selection of organic wines.

Info: 10th/Métro Bonne Nouvelle, Poissonière or Château d'Eau. 43 rue des Petites Ecuries (between rue du Faubourg Poissonière and rue d'Hauteville). Tel. 01/42.46.43.55. Closed Sat. and Sun. www.vivantparis.com. Moderate.

Le Vingt Heures Vin *Map p. 126 #5*

The owner of this vibrant wine bar in Montmartre (there's another location in the 11th at 2 rue des Goncourt) is a wine buff who'll help you with your selection. Relax over a glass or bottle of wine with bread, cheese, *charcuterie*, small plates, or a salad (the "Emile Buisson" vegetarian salad is a good choice). Try *la tartine chic* with ham, tomato, basil, and cheese. Popular late at night. *Info*: 18th/Métro Abbesses. 15/17 rue Joseph de Maistre. Tel. 09/54.66.50.67. Open Tue-Sun 7 p.m. to 1 a.m. www.vingtheuresvin.com. Moderate.

HISTORIC RESTAURANTS

Recognized for its food traditions the world over, Paris is filled with restaurants and bistros—many of which have survived and flourished for over one hundred years. Make a point of dining in at least one of these historic settings to experience the culinary heritage of this great city.

Bofinger *Map p. 127 #11*

Beautiful glass-roofed brasserie with lots of stained glass and brass, located between the place des Vosges and the place de la Bastille. It's the oldest Alsatian brasserie in Paris, and still serves traditional dishes like *choucroute* (sauerkraut) and large platters of shellfish. *Info*: 4th/Métro Bastille. 5 rue de la Bastille. Tel. 01/42.72.87.82. Open daily. www.bofingerparis.com. Moderate - Expensive. Across the street and less expensive is **Le Petit Bofinger**, 6 rue de la Bastille, Tel. 01/42.72.05.23.

Bouillon Racine *Map p. 125 #12*

Brasserie in a historic building with beautiful Art Nouveau decor. Try one of the soups offered such as *crème de potiron et châtaigne* (cream of pumpkin and chestnut). *Info*: 6th/Métro Cluny-La Sorbonne or Odéon. 3 rue Racine (near blvd. Saint-Michel). Tel. 01/44.32.15.60. Open daily. www.bouillon-racine.com. Moderate.

Brasserie Balzar *Map p. 125 #13*

This Latin Quarter brasserie opened in 1898 and serves traditional French cuisine. It's known for its *poulet rôti* (roast chicken), onion soup and "colorful" waiters. *Info*: 5th/Métro Cluny-La Sorbonne. 49 rue des Ecoles (near blvd. Saint-Michel). Tel. 01/43.54.13.67. Open daily until midnight. www.brasseriebalzar.com. Moderate - Expensive.

Brasserie Flo *Map p. 124 #18*

Alsatian food and Parisian atmosphere at this 1886 brasserie, on a passageway in an area not frequented by tourists. Jam-packed with some of the strangest people you'll see in Paris, and getting there is half the fun. Try the *gigot d'agneau* (leg of lamb). *Info*: 10th/ Métro Château d'Eau. 7 cour des Petites-Écuries (enter from 63 rue du Fg-St-Denis). Tel. 01/47.70.13.59. Open daily. www.floparis.com. Expensive.

Chartier *Map p. 124 #19*

Traditional Paris soup kitchen. The *tripes à la mode de Caen* is a frequent special of the day (we passed on that). Lots of tourists, and you may be seated with strangers. Expect to wait in line. You're coming

Great place for a cheap lunch.

here for the experience, not necessarily for the food. *Info*: 9th/Métro Grands Boulevards. 7 rue du Faubourg-Montmartre (off of blvd. Poissonnière). Tel. 01/47.70.86.29. Open daily 11:30 a.m. to 10 p.m. www.restaurant-chartier.com. Inexpensive.

Chez Marianne *Map p. 124 #20*

Popular take-away deli (you can also eat here, but it's difficult to get a table) known for its authentic Jewish and Eastern European specialties, especially *falafel*. Located in the heart of the Marais. *Info*: 4th/Métro St-Paul. 2 rue des Hospitalières-St-Gervais (at rue des Rosiers). Tel. 01/42.72.18.86. Open daily. No credit cards. Inexpensive.

La Closerie des Lilas *Map p. 125 #14*
Lenin and Trotsky are among those who have visited this historic
café. There's a terrace, piano bar, brasserie (moderate) and
restaurant (expensive). The brasserie is known for its *steak tartare*.
Info: 14th/Métro Raspail or Vavin. 171 boulevard du Montparnasse
(near blvd. Saint-Michel). Tel. 01/40.51.34.50. Open daily.
www.closeriedeslilas.fr. Moderate - Expensive.

La Coupole *Map p. 125 #15*
A Montparnasse institution since the days of Picasso, this noisy
brasserie known for its *huîtres* (oysters) is a favorite among tourists.
Info: 14th/Métro Vavin. 102 boulevard du Montparnasse (at rue
Vavin). Tel. 01/43.20.14.20. Open daily. www.lacoupole-paris.com.
Expensive.

Le Grand Colbert *Map p. 124 #21*
Housed in a restored historic building, serving traditional brasserie cuisine. Known for its seafood tray. This stunning restaurant
was featured in the movie *Something's Gotta Give*, so lots of tourists. *Info*: 2nd/Métro Bourse. 2 rue Vivienne (near the Place des
Victoires). Tel. 01/42.86.87.88. Closed part of Aug.
www.legrandcolbert.fr. Moderate - Expensive.

Aux Lyonnais *Map p. 124 #22*
This beautiful century-old bistro has been renovated and serves the
cuisine of Lyon. Try the *sanglier* (wild boar) when available. The
wine of choice is Beaujolais. It's part of the Alain Ducasse group.
Info: 2nd/Métro Bourse. 32 rue Saint-Marc (off of rue de Richelieu).
Tel. 01/42.96.65.04. Closed Sat. (lunch), Sun. and Mon.
www.auxlyonnais.com Expensive.

Ma Bourgogne *Map p. 127 #12*
This café/restaurant in the place des
Vosges (the oldest square in Paris)
serves traditional Parisian cuisine

Ma Bourgogne another favorite.

and specializes in *poulet rôti* (roast chicken). Good salads. Open for
breakfast, lunch, and dinner. *Info*: 4th/Métro St-Paul. 19 place des
Vosges. Tel. 01/42.78.44.64. Open daily. No credit cards.
www.ma-bourgogne.fr. Moderate.

Perraudin *Map p. 125 #16*

You'll get to know your fellow diners at this inexpensive bistro serving traditional Parisian cuisine just steps from the Panthéon. Try the *magret de canard au miel et romarin* (duck breast w/honey and rosemary sauce). *Info*: 5th/Métro Cluny-La Sorbonne. 157 rue Saint-Jacques (near rue Soufflot). Tel. 01/46.33.15.75. Open daily. www.restaurant-perraudin.com. Inexpensive - Moderate.

Polidor *Map p. 125 #17*

You'll sit at communal tables at this popular old-fashioned bistro serving traditional cuisine such as *pintade* (guinea hen). French comfort food. *Info*: 6th/Métro Odéon. 41 rue Monsieur-le-Prince (near rue Racine). Tel. 01/43.26.95.34. Open daily. No reservations. No credit cards. www.polidor.com. Inexpensive - Moderate.

Terminus Nord *Map p. 124 #23*

What a great way to arrive in (or depart from) Paris! This large, bustling brasserie near the Gare du Nord is just so Parisian with its mahogany bar, polished wood and beveled glass. Seafood platters, *bouillabaisse*, and duck breast are the featured dishes. *Info*: 10th/Métro Gare du Nord. 23 rue de Dunkerque. Tel. 01/42.85.05.15. Open daily. www.terminusnord.com. Expensive.

Le Train Bleu *Map p. 127 #13*

Beautiful Restauran

Forget all the food you've eaten in train stations. It's delicious here. The setting, with its murals of the French-speaking world, is spectacular. A great place to have a drink. *Info*: 12th/Métro Gare-de-Lyon. 20 boulevard Diderot (in the Gare de Lyon train station). Tel. 01/43.43.09.06. Open daily. www.le-train-bleu.com. Expensive.

Willi's Wine Bar *Map p. 124 #24*

British owners serving specialties with Mediterranean influences. A great wine list, and a favorite of many travelers to Paris. *Info*: 1st/Métro Bourse. 13 rue des Petits-Champs (near rue Vivienne). Tel. 01/42.61.05.09. Closed Sun. and part of Aug. www.williswinebar.com. Moderate.

⚞ PLACES TO DRINK ⚟

More wine bars are listed above in the Places to Eat section of this guide.

L'Art Source

This attractive wine bar with stone walls and beamed ceiling is located on a pedestrian street off of rue Montorgueil. The helpful English-speaking staff will guide you through the wines by the glass. Small plates offered include mini-burgers and *ceviche*. In warm weather, there's a small and comfortable area in front where you can sit outside. Great choice for a late-night drink and snack. *Info*: 2nd/Métro Etienne Marcel. 6 rue Marie Stuart (off of rue Montorgueil). Tel. 09/82.55.00.49. Open Tue-Sat 6:30 p.m. to 2 a.m. www.lartsource.com. Inexpensive-Moderate.

Le Baron Rouge

Have a glass of wine (some right from the barrel) at this neighborhood wine bar. You'll sit at communal tables. Try the *charcuterie*, cheese platters, and oysters (on weekends). It's especially busy on Sunday afternoons. *Info*: 12th/Métro Ledru-Rollin. 1 rue Théophile Roussel. Tel. 01/43.43.14.32. Closed Sun (dinner) and Mon. Moderate.

Café de la Nouvelle Mairie

This bustling wine bar/café near the Panthéon serves classic French food and small plates. There are about twenty wines served by the glass (starting at €4) and many are organic. Especially nice in the summer. Friendly English-speaking staff. Always packed elbow-to-elbow. *Info*: 5th/Métro Cardinal Lemoine or RER B Luxembourg. 19 rue des Fossés Saint Jacques. Tel. 01/44.07.04.41. Closed most weekends. Inexpensive-Moderate.

Coinstot Vino

Guillaume Dupré runs this casual wine bar located in the passage des Panoramas. In addition to the superior wine list, you can order small plates (such as wild bass on endive) or select from a few main courses. *Info*: 2nd/Métro Grands Boulevards. 26 passage des Panoramas. Tel. 01/44.82.08.54. Closed Sunday. www.coinstot-vino.com. Moderate.

Le Dokhan

An elegant champagne bar where you
can enjoy it by the flute or by the bottle.
Try the three champagnes for €30.
Info: 16th/Métro Trocadéro
117 rue Lauriston (in Trocadéro Dokhan's Hôtel)
Tel. 01/53.65.66.99. Open daily.

Coupe de Champagne

Le Garde Robe

This wine bar in the residential 17th features mostly organic wines
(with an emphasis on white wines from Loire) and has a knowledge-
able staff. Delicious *charcuterie* and cheese plates. Its other location
is in the 1st at 41 rue de l'Arbre Sec. *Info*: 17th/Métro Rome or La
Fourche. 4 rue Bridaine. Tel. 01/44.90.05.04. Open daily. Moderate.

Au Lapin Agile

You'll hear French folk tunes at this shuttered cottage at the picturesque intersection of rue des Saules and rue St-Vincent. It was
once frequented by Picasso. You'll sit at small wooden tables and
listen to *chansonniers* (singers). Truly a Parisian experience. *Info*:
18th/Métro Lamarck-Caulaincourt. Intersection of rue des Saules
and rue St-Vincent. Tel. 01/46.06.85.87. Open Tue-Sun 9pm-1am.
Closed Mon. Admission: €28 (includes a drink). No credit cards.
Reservations can be made at www.au-lapin-agile.com. *Map p. 126*

Le Trésor

Cocktails served both inside and outside at tables along this lovely,
flowered street in the heart of the Marais. Great people-watching.
Info: 4th/Métro Hôtel de Ville or St-Paul. 5-7 rue du Trésor (off of
rue Vieille du Temple). Tel. 01/42.71.35.17. Open daily.

En Vrac

The name means "in bulk" and you can have bottles (with stoppers)
filled with your choice of wines to go. At €4 to €8 a bottle, that's
quite a deal. The bar is lined with wine-filled steel tanks. There's a
plat du jour along with cheese plates, charcuterie, and sandwiches
made to order. *Info*: 18th/Métro Marx Dormoy. 2 rue de l'Olive (at
the corner of 92 rue Riquet). Tel. 01/53.26.03.94. Open daily 10am-
midnight. www.vinenvrac.fr/en. Inexpensive.

Bakeries (Boulangeries), Chocolate Shops (Chocolateries), Pastry Shops (Pâtisseries) and Candy Stores (Confiseries)

Kayser

Excellent *baguettes*, specialty breads like the coarse and hearty *pain au levain*, and delicious *pain au chocolate*. *Info*: 5th/Métro Maubert-Mutualité. 8 and 14 rue Monge (other locations throughout the city). Tel. 01/44.07.01.42 and 01/44.07.17.81. Closed Tue. (8 rue Monge). Closed Mon. (14 rue Monge). www.maison-kayser.com

Lenôtre

Café, kitchen shop (everything from pots and pans to wine) and cooking school all in the elegant glass-and-stone Pavillon Elysée. Lenôtre has many other shops in Paris. *Info*: 8th/Métro Champs-Elysées – Clemenceau. 10 avenue des Champs-Elysées. Tel. 01/42.65.85.10. Closed part of Aug. www.lenotre.fr

Marquise de Sévigné

A French "luxury" (their word) chocolate maker since 1898. Packaged in signature blue boxes. *Info*: 8th/Métro Madeleine. 11 place de la Madeleine. Tel. 01/42.65.19.47. Closed Sun.

The marquise de Sévigné lived in what is now the Carnavalet

La Maison du Chocolat

Every chocolate lover should visit. There are several shops in the city, including 8 boulevard de la Madeleine (9th/Métro Madeleine). *Info*: 8th/Métro Ternes. 225 rue du Faubourg-St-Honoré. Tel. 01/42.27.39.44. Open daily.

Patrick Roger

Patrick Roger's friendly shop on the boulevard St-Germain-des-Prés has excellent chocolates packaged in green boxes that make great gifts and are easy to pack to take home. Other locations include 45 avenue Victor Hugo (16th/Métro Kleber. Tel. 01/45.01.66.71. Closed Sun.). *Info*: 6th/Métro Odéon. 108 boulevard St-Germain-des-Prés. Tel. 01/43.29.38.42. Open daily. www.patrickroger.com

Stohrer

The Parisian favorite of *baba au rhum* (spongecake soaked in rum) was invented at this *pâtisserie* in the Montorgueil quarter. *Info*: 2nd/ Métro Les Halles. 51 rue Montorgueil. Tel. 01/42.33.38.20. Closed part of Aug. www.stohrer.fr

A La Mère de Famille

The oldest *confiserie* in Paris (since 1761). Locations throughout the city. *Info*: 9th/Métro Le Peletier or Cadet. 33 and 35 rue du Faubourg-Montmartre. Tel. 01/47.70.83.69. Closed part of Aug. www.lameredefamille.com

Cheese Shops (Fromageries)

Alléosse

Cheese is like gold to the French. Charles de Gaulle is reported to have said, "How can anyone govern a nation that has 246 different kinds of cheese?" This cheese shop on a busy market street serves rare cheeses from throughout France. *Info*: 17th/Métro Ternes. 13 rue Poncelet. Tel. 01/46.22.50.45. Closed Sun. (afternoon) and Mon. www.fromage-alleosse.com

Barthélemy

This small cheese shop on the Left Bank is where Parisians shop for their cheese. When you walk in, you're overtaken by the intense smell of some of the best cheeses available in France. *Info*: 7th/ Métro Rue du Bac. 51 rue de Grenelle. Tel. 01/42.22.82.24. Closed Sun., Mon. and Aug.

Specialty Food Stores (Épiceries)

Albert Ménès

Gourmet food shop that specializes in food from the provinces. *Info*: 8th/Métro Madeleine or St-Augustin. 41 boulevard Malesherbes. Tel. 01/42.66.95.63. Closed Sat., Sun., Mon. (morning), and mid-July to mid-Aug.

Boutique Maille

Boutique mustard shop on the
place de la Madeleine.
Info: 8th/Métro Madeleine.
6 place de la Madeleine.
Tel. 01/40.15.06.00.
Closed Sun.
www.maille.com

Caviar Kaspia

Caviar, blinis and salmon. There's also a restaurant upstairs.
Info: 8th/Métro Madeleine. 17 place de la Madeleine.
Tel. 01/42.65.66.21. Closed Sun. www.kaspia.fr

Fauchon

Deli and grocery known for its huge
selection of canned food, baked goods
and alcohol. The store is a must for
those wanting to bring back French
specialties. *Info*: 8th/Métro Madeleine.
26 place de la Madeleine.
Tel. 01/70.39.38.00. Closed Sun.
www.fauchon.com

Do not touch the food! A clerk must get it for you.

Gourmet Lafayette

This department store has a huge gourmet-food section, with tasting bars, restaurants, and deli counters. *Info*: 8th/Métro Chaussée-d'Antin. 40 boulevard Hausmann (in the Galeries Lafayette department store). Tel. 01/42.82.34.56. Closed Sun.

La Grande Épicerie

The *ultimate* grocery store (with wine cellar and carry-out). Don't miss it! *Info*: 7th/Métro Sèvres Babylone. 38 rue Sèvres (in Au Bon Marché department store). Tel. 01/44.39.81.00. Closed Sun.
www.lagrandeepicerie.com

Hédiard

Food store/spice shop that has been open since the 1850s, similar to Fauchon, with an on-site restaurant. *Info*: 8th/Métro Madeleine
21 place de la Madeleine. Tel. 01/43.12.88.88. Closed Sun.

La Maison du Miel

This food store located around the corner from Fauchon offers everything made from honey (from sweets to soap). *Info*: 9th/Métro Madeleine or Opéra. 24 rue Vignon. Tel. 01/47.42.26.70. Closed Sun. www.maisondumiel.fr

Oliviers & Co.

Olive oils from around the Mediterranean at several lovely shops:
3rd/60 rue Vielle du Temple,
4th/81 rue St Louis en l'Ile, 5th/128 rue Mouffetard,
12th/Bercy Village, 15th/85 rue du Commerce, and
18th/18 rue Lepic. www.oliviers-co.com

G. Detou

You'll find a little of everything food-related at this shop near the rue Montorgueil (one of the best fish and meat markets in the city). Great gifts to take home include dried mushrooms, chocolates, olive oil, glazed chestnuts, and canned *foie gras*. You can also visit their kitchenware shop **A. Simon** nearby at 48 and 52 rue Montmartre. *Info*: 2nd/Métro Etienne Marcel. 58 rue Tiquetonne. Tel. 01/42.36.54.67. Closed Sun.

Wine Stores (Caves) and Wine Tastings

La Dernière Goutte

Located in an old vaulted room. The *The last drop.* owners are charming and friendly, and they frequently have wine tastings. *Info*: 6th/Métro St-Germain-des-Prés. 6 rue de Bourbon-le-Château..Tel. 01/43.29.11.62. www.laderniéregoutte.net

Les Caves Taillevent

This wine shop is associated with the well-known Taillevent restaurant and is said to have over 500,000 bottles of wine starting at around 5 euros. You'll be amazed at the cost of some selections. *Info*: 8th/Métro Charles-de-Gaulle-Étoile or Saint-Philippe-du-Roule. 228 rue du Faubourg-Saint-Honoré. Tel. 01/45.61.14.09. Open 10 a.m. to 7:30 p.m. Closed Sun. and Aug. www.taillevent.com

Les Caves Augé

Famous wine shop since 1850 offering everything from prestige wines to foreign vintages. *Info*: 8th/Métro Saint-Augustin. 116 boulevard Haussmann. Tel. 01/45.22.16.97. Closed Sun. and Mon. (morning).

Lavinia

The largest wine shop in Paris with 2000 foreign wines, 3000 French wines, and 1000 spirits, priced from 4 to 3600 euros. Drink any bottle from the shop at the wine bar. Lunch served (with wine, of course). *Info*: 1st/Métro Madeleine. 3-5 boulevard de la Madeleine. Tel. 01/42.97.20.27. (restaurant). Tel. 01/492.97.20.20 (shop). Open 10 a.m. until 8:30 p.m. Closed Sun.

Ô Chateau

"Coming to Paris and not tasting good French wines is like going to the U.S. and not trying a good burger," says Olivier Magny. This young French sommelier will guide you through a fun, informative, and relaxing wine tasting. From €30. The wine bar is the largest in Paris. The restaurant/wine bar offers a three-course menu (€39), a tasting menu (€69 – including three glasses of wine), and a premium tasting menu (€95 – including three glasses of premium wine). *Info*: 1st/Métro Louvre-Rivoli. 68 rue Jean-Jacques Rousseau. Tel. 01/44.73.97.80. Closed Sun. www.o-chateau.com

Legrand Filles et Fils

In the elegant Galerie Vivienne, this wine bar and shop has been run by the Legrand family for over three generations. Sandwiches, salads and cheese platters. A great place for a light lunch. *Info*: 2nd/Métro Bourse. 1 rue de la Banque. Tel. 01/42.60.07.12. Open 10 a.m. to 7 p.m. Closed Sun. www.caves-legrand.com

Nicolas

Located upstairs from the Nicolas wine shop. You can buy a bottle of wine at the shop and have it served with your meal. The menu is limited, but the wines sold by the glass are inexpensive. There are over 200 wine stores located throughout Paris. *Info*: 8th/Métro Madeleine. 31 Place de la Madeleine. Tel. 01/44.51.90.22. Open 9:30 a.m. to 8:00 p.m. Closed Sun. www.nicolas.com

Ladurée

Elegant *salon de thé* and pastry shop
near place de la Madeleine. Try a
macaron. Other locations throughout
the city, including 75 avenue des
Champs-Elysées. *Info*: 8th/Métro
Madeleine. 16-18 rue Royale. Tel. 01/42.60.21.79.
Open daily. www.laduree.fr

Mariage-Frères

400 types of teas served in elegant
rooms serving light meals and
weekend brunch. *Info*: 6th/Métro
Odéon or Saint-Michel
13 rue des Grands Augustins
(other locations throughout the city)
Tel. 01/40.51.82.50. Open daily.
www.mariagefreres.com

Dammann Frères

Are you a secret tea-totaller? This tea shop is located on the place
des Vosges. Walk in and you will find yourself surrounded by walls
lined with shelves holding black canisters filled with rare teas,
which you can sample before you purchase. The elegant boxes make
great gifts or souvenirs. *Info*: 4th/Métro St-Paul or Bastille. 15 place
des Vosges. Tel. 01/44.54.04.88. Open daily. www.dammann.fr

Organic, Vegan, Vegetarian, Gluten-Free, and Lactose-Free

Paris is embracing the organic-food movement. There are several
grocery stores featuring organic products (Closed Sun.):
BioCoop, throughout Paris, including 44 bd. de Grenelle, 15th/Métro
Bir-Hakeim or Dupleix, www.biocoop.fr.
Naturalia, throughout Paris, including 11 rue Renard, 4th/Métro
Hôtel de Ville, www.naturalia.fr.

There are also several organic outdoor markets, including:

Marché bio Raspail, boulevard Raspail, 6th/Métro Rennes (Sun.)

Marché bio Brancusi, place Brancusi, 14th/Métro Gaité (Sat.)

Marché bio Batignolles, boulevard des Batignolles, 17th/Métro Place de Clichy (Sat.)

Le So

This organic restauraunt is in a modern space with designer chairs and tables. You might try the juicy tofu burger or *poulet fermier* (free-range chicken). There's a very popular brunch on Sat. and Sun. *Info*: 2nd/Métro Bourse or Sentier. 93 rue Montmartre (at rue Paul-Lelong). Tel. 01/40.28.02.83. Closed Sun. (dinner) and Mon. (dinner). www.le-so.fr. Moderate.

Noglu

This gluten-free restaurant (and take-out) also offers some lactose-free dishes. The menu changes daily and features everything from *cabaillaud* (cod) to pizza. It's located in the lovely Passage des Panoramas. Excellent desserts. *Info*: 2nd/Métro Bourse or Grands Boulevards. 16 Passage des Panoramas. Tel. 01/40.26.41.24. Closed Sun.. www.noglu.fr. Moderate.

Soya

You'll find inventive vegetarian dishes at this small, intimate restaurant. Try the lasagna stuffed with tofu. Excellent list of organic wines. *Info*: 11th/Métro République. 20 rue de la Pierre Levée (off of rue de la Fontaine-au-Roi). Tel. 01/48.06.33.02. Closed Sun. (dinner) and Mon. Moderate.

Le Potager du Marais

This small vegetarian/vegan restaurant is located near the Centre Pompidou. Try the *soupe à l'oignon gratinée* (French onion soup). *Info*: 3rd/Métro Rambuteau. 24 rue Rambuteau (between rue Beaubourg and rue du Temple). Tel. 01/57.40.98.57. Closed Mon. (dinner) and Tue. Moderate.

Café Beaubourg

Looking onto the Centre Pompidou
and packed with an artsy crowd.
We meet friends here every year
and always have a great time!
Info: 4th/Métro Rambuteau. 43
rue St-Merri. Tel. 01/48.87.63.96.
Open daily 8 a.m. to 2 a.m.
www.cafebeaubourg.com

Café Les Deux Magots

If you're a tourist, you'll fit right in at one of Hemingway's favorite
spots. We don't really recommend that you eat here (there is a limited menu), but have a drink and enjoy the great people-watching.
Info: 6th/Métro Saint-Germain-des-Prés. 6 place Saint-Germain-des-Prés. Tel. 01/45.48.55.25. Open daily 7:30 a.m. to 1 a.m.
www.cafelesdeuxmagots.com

Café de Flore

Another famous café and a favorite of tourists and Parisians alike
(next door to Les Deux Magots). *Info*: 6th/Métro Saint-Germain-des-Prés. 172 boulevard. Saint-Germain-des-Prés.
Tel. 01/45.48.55.26. Open daily 7 a.m. to 2 a.m.
www.cafedeflore.fr

Café de l'Industrie

Near the Opéra Bastille, this inexpensive
café features a limited menu, a diverse wine
list, and an interesting crowd.
Info: 11th/Métro Bastille.
16 rue St-Sabin. Tel. 01/47.00.13.53.
Open daily 9 a.m. to 2 a.m.
www.cafedelindustrieparis.fr

Café L'Été en Pente Douce

Interesting and picturesque
Montmartre café near Sacré-Coeur.
Take a break here after you climb
the steps to Sacré-Coeur! *Info*: 18th/
Métro Château-Rouge or Anvers.
23 rue Muller. Tel. 01/42.64.02.67.

L'ete en pente douce ~ Summer on a gentle slope.

Open daily. If you're facing Sacré-Coeur, take the steps down to your
right (rue Maurice-Utrillo) and at the bottom is rue Muller and the
café. *Map p. 126 #1*

Café de la Paix

Famous café (not really known for its food). Popular with tourists. Another spot for outdoor people-watching (and the inside is
stunnning). *Info*: 9th/Métro Opéra. 5 place de l'Opéra.
Tel. 01/40.07.36.36. Open daily 7 a.m. to midnight
www.cafedelapaix.fr

Café Marly

This café overlooks the pyramid
at the Louvre and no place in
Paris has a better setting. Standard
bistro fare served by waiters in suits.
It's a great place for a relaxing lunch,
or come here after dinner and end
your day with a glass of champagne.
Definitely worth the cost!

we LoVE the pyramids.

Info: 1st/Métro Musée du Louvre/Palais-Royal.
93 rue de Rivoli. Tel. 01/49.26.06.60.
Open daily 8 a.m. to 2 a.m.
www.cafe-marly.com

Pause Café

Popular café specializing in *tourtes*.
Info: 11th/Métro Ledru-Rollin.
41 rue de Charonne.
Tel. 01/48.06.80.33.
Open Mon. - Sat. 8 a.m. to 2 a.m.,
Sun 9 a.m. to 8 p.m.

If you're looking for a comprehensive guide to speaking French, this is not the right place. What follows are simply a few tips for speaking French and a very brief pronunciation guide.

It is always good to learn a few polite terms so that you can excuse yourself when you've stepped on the foot of an elderly lady or spilled your drink down the back of the gentleman in front of you. It's also just common courtesy to greet the people you meet in your hotel, in shops and restaurants in their own language.

If a word ends in a consonant and that word is followed by a word that starts in a vowel, the consonant is linked to the vowel. So, **vous avez** (you have) is pronounced voozavay. And the final consonant in a word is silent (unless followed by an e).

a like in far
e like in open
é and ez like the a in rate
è like the e in bet
ê like eh as in *crêpe*
i like the i in machine
o like the o in not
ô like the o in wrote
u round your lips as to say oh, but say ee
an, am, en, em, ant, ent like the a in wand
au, eau like the o in okay
er at the end of a word sounds like the ay in day
in, im, ain, aim like the a in sank
ou like the oo in cool
oi like the wa in water
que like the cu in curve
qui like kee

un is pronounced uhn
c like a k before a, o, u and consonants
c like an s before e and i
ch like sh
ç like the s in simple
g before a, o and u like in good
g like the s in pleasure before i and e
gn like the ny in canyon
h is always silent
j like the s in measure
r like an r being swallowed
s like the s in step but when between vowels, it's pronounced like a z
ss like an s
zh like the s in measure

This is a brief listing of some familiar English foods and food-related words that you may need in a restaurant setting. It is followed by a list of phrases that may come in handy. There are also some pronunciation prompts. They aren't all exactly right, but they're close enough to get you what you need.

allergic, allergique *anchois~*
anchovies, anchois *an-shwa*
appetizer, hors-d'oeuvre
apple, pomme
artichoke, artichaut
ashtray, cendrier
asparagus, aspèrge
bacon, lard (lardons)
baked, au four/cuit au four
banana, banane
beans, fève
beef, boeuf
beefsteak, bifteck/steak
beer, bière
beverages, boissons
bill, l'addition
bitter, amer
boiled, bouilli
bottle (half), demi-bouteille
bottle, bouteille *boutielle~*
bowl, bol *boo-tay*
braised, braisé
bread, pain
bread roll, petit pain

breakfast, petit déjeuner
broth, consommé
butter, beurre
cabbage, chou
cake, gâteau
candle, chandelle/bougie
carrot, carotte
cereal, céréale(s)
chair, chaise
check, chèque
cheers, santé
cheese, fromage
cherry, cerise
chicken, poulet
chicken breast, suprême de volaille
chops, côtelettes, côtes
clams, palourdes
cocktail, cocktail
cod, morue
coffee, café
coffee (American-style), café américain
coffee w/milk, café crème/un crème (*café au lait* if you want a lot of milk)
coffee (black), café noir
coffee (decaf), déca/décafféiné
cold, froid
corn, maïs
cover charge, couvert
credit card, carte de crédit
cucumber, concombre
cup, tasse
custard, crème anglaise
dessert, dessert
dinner, dîner

dish (plate), assiette. A main
dish is *plat principal*
drink, boisson
duck, canard
eggs, oeufs
espresso, café express/un
express
fish, poisson
fish soup, bouillabaisse (the
famous seafood stew)
fork, fourchette
french fries, frites (pommes
frites)
fresh, fraîche/frais
fried, frit
fruit, fruits
game, gibier
garlic, ail
gin, gin
glass, verre
goat, chèvre
goose, oie
grapefruit, pamplemousse
grapes, raisin
green beans, haricots verts
grilled, grillé
ham (cooked), jambon (cuit)
ham (cured), jambon (de
Parme and de Bayonne)
hamburger, hamburger
honey, miel
hot, chaud
ice, glaçon
ice cream, glace
ice (on the rocks), avec des
glaçons
ice water, l'eau glacée

included, compris
ketchup, ketchup
knife, couteau
kosher, casher/kascher
lamb, agneau
large, grand
lemon, citron
lettuce, laitue
little, petit/peu de...
liver, foie
lobster, homard
loin, longe (pork)/aloyau (beef)
lunch, déjeuner
match, allumette
mayonnaise, mayonnaise
meat, viande
medium (cooked), à point
melon, melon
menu, carte
milk, lait
Lait écrémé is skim milk
and *lait entier*, whole milk
mineral water, eau minérale
mineral water (sparkling),
eau minérale (gazeuse)
**mineral water (w/out carbon-
ation),** eau minérale plate (non
gazeuse)
mixed, mélange, mixte,
mesclun (salad greens)
mushrooms, champignons
mussels, moules
mustard, moutarde
napkin, serviette
noodles, pâtes/nouilles
nuts, noix
octopus, poulpes

handwritten annotations:
couteau – coo.
ail ~ aye
déjeuner ~ day- juh-
chaud ~
froid
show ~
FWA

oil, huile
olive oil, huile d'olive
olives, olives
omelette, omelette
on the rocks (w/ ice), avec des glaçons
onions, oignons *oignons ~*
orange, orange *ON-yone*
orange juice, jus d'orange
overdone, trop cuit *huîtres ~*
oysters, huîtres *weeT-RAH*
partridge, perdrix
pastry, pâtisserie
peaches, pêches
pears, poires
peas, petits pois
pepper (black), poivre
peppers (sweet), poivrons
perch, perche
pineapple, ananas
plate (dish), assiette
please, s'il vous plaît
plums, prunes
poached, poché
pork, porc
potatoes, pommes de terre
poultry, volaille
prawns, grosses crevettes/ langoustines
quail, caille
rabbit, lapin
rare, saignant
raspberry, framboises
receipt, note/reçu
rice, riz
roast, rôti
rolls, petits pains

salad, salade
salmon, saumon
salt, sel
sandwich, sandwich(e)
sauce, sauce
sautéed, sauté
scallops, coquilles (Saint-Jacques) *brouille ~*
scrambled, brouillé *brew-ee*
seafood, fruits de mer
seasonings, condiments/ assaisonnement
shellfish, crustacés
shrimp, crevettes
small, petit
smoked, fumé
snails, escargots
sole, sole
soup, soupe
spaghetti, spaghetti
sparkling (wine), champagne
specialty, spécialité *epicé ~*
spicy, épicé *AY-PEE-SAY*
spinach, épinards
spoon, cuiller/cuillère
squid, calmar/calamar
steak, steak/bifteck
steamed, vapeur
stew, ragoût
strawberries, fraises
sugar, sucre
sugar substitute, édulcorant/de l'aspartam
supper, dîner
sweet, doux/sucré
table, table
tea, thé

tea w/lemon, thé citron
tea w/milk, thé au lait
thank you, merci
tip, pourboire
toast, pain grillé *grillé ~ grec-AY*
tomato, tomate
toothpick, cure-dents
trout, truite
tuna, thon
turkey, dindon/dinde
utensil, couvert
veal, veau
vegetable, légume
vegetarian, végétarien
venison, venaison
vinegar, vinaigre
vodka, vodka
waiter, monsieur (never *garçon*)
waitress, madame or mademoiselle
water, eau
watermelon, pastèque
well done, bien cuit. Very well done is *très bien cuit*
whipped cream, crème chantilly *(shan-tee-ee)*
wine, vin
wine list, carte des vins
wine (red), vin rouge
wine (rosé), vin rosé
wine (white), vin blanc
with, avec
without, sans
yogurt, yaourt

Helpful Phrases

please, s'il vous plaît
thank you, merci
yes, oui
no, non
good morning, bonjour
good afternoon, bonjour
good evening, bonsoir
good night, bonne nuit
goodbye, au revoir

Do you speak English?, parlez-vous anglais?
I don't speak French, je ne parle pas français
excuse me, pardon
I don't understand, je ne comprends pas
I'd like a table, je voudrais une table
I'd like to reserve a table, je voudrais réserver une table
for one person, pour une personne *–UNE – deh*
for two, pour deux *– deh*
--trois (3) *–Twa*
--quatre (4) *– CaT*
--cinq (5) *– Sank*
--six (6) *– see*
--sept (7) *~ seT*
--huit (8) *– weeT*
--neuf (9) *– nurf*
--dix (10) *– deece*

this evening, ce soir

tomorrow, demain

near the window, près de la fenêtre

with a view, avec vue

outside on the patio, sur la terrasse

no smoking, non-fumeur. As of January 2008,
   smoking is banned in all restaurants

where is?, où est

where are?, où sont

the bathrooms, les toilettes

the bill, l'addition

a mistake (error), une erreur

Is service included?, Le service est-il compris?

Do you accept credit cards?, acceptez-vous les cartes de crédit

traveler's checks, chèques de voyage

How much is it?, c'est combien?

What is this?, qu'est-ce que c'est?

I did not order this, ce n'est pas ce que j'ai commandé

This is, c'est

—too, trop   —Trow

—cold, froid   — FWA

—hot, chaud   —SHow

—not fresh, n'est pas frais   — NAY PAH FRAIS

—rare, saignant   —SANE-YANT

—undercooked, pas assez cuit   — PAH AH SAY CWEE

—overcooked, trop cuit   TROW CWEE

—delicious, délicieux

I am a vegetarian, Je suis végétarien(ne)

without meat, pas de viande/sans viande

closed, fermé

Monday, lundi   Lundee

Tuesday, mardi   Mardee

Wednesday, mercredi   Mare KRA dee

Thursday, jeudi   Juh dee

Friday, vendredi   Yawndradee

Saturday, samedi   Samahdee

Sunday, dimanche   Dee mansh

MENU READER

FRENCH TO ENGLISH

AAAAA, the seal of approval of
*l'Association Amicale des Amateurs
d'Andouillettes Authentiques.*
Only in France would they have an
association for devotees of
andouillette (tripe sausage)

*In French
Amateur mean
"Lover of "*

abats, abattis, organ meats

abricot, apricot

acras/accras, *beignets,* usually stuffed
w/seafood, found in the French West Indies

acidulé, acidic

addition (l'addition), check/bill

affinée, aged

agneau, lamb

agneau de lait, milk-fed lamb

agneau pré-salé, lamb grazed on salt marshes

agrumes, citrus fruits

Agrumes.

aiglefin, haddock

aïgo bouido, garlic soup (means "boiled water")

aigre, sour

aigre-doux, sweet and sour

aigrelette, a sour sauce

aiguebelle, herbal after-dinner drink similar to *Chartreuse*

aiguillette, thin slice. *Aiguillette de boeuf* are slices of steak

ail, garlic

aile, wing of poultry

aile de raie, ray fin (a kite-shaped
fish also called skate)

*Aile is used
to mean
white meat.*

aile et cuisse, *aile*: literally wing,
it means white meat in fowl
cuisse: literally leg, it means dark meat in fowl

ailerons, wings

aillade, garlic mayonnaise (see *aïoli*)

aillade gasconne, veal w/garlic found in Southwest France

aïoli/ailloli, garlic mayonnaise. Found in many
provençal dishes

aïoli garni, *aïoli* served w/boiled food, salt cod, vegetables and eggs

airelle, cranberry

à la, à l', au, aux, in the manner of, in, with

à la carte, side dishes (each item ordered separately)

albert, a sauce of egg yolk, cream, horseradish, shallots and mustard

albuféra, *béchamel* sauce w/sweet peppers

alcool, alcohol

algues, seaweed

ali baba, spongecake soaked in rum

aligot, garlic mashed potatoes w/cheese

alimentation, food/food store

allumettes, puff pastry or potato strips

alose, shad (fish)

alouette, lark

alouette sans tête, rolled veal slice
    stuffed w/garlic and minced meat

aloyau, sirloin

Alsace, located in the northeast corner of France (along the
    German border); one of France's wine regions specializing
    in white wines such as Gewürztraminer, Riesling, Pinot Gris,
    Pinot Blanc, Pinot Noir and Sylvaner

alsacienne, alsacien/usually garnished w/sausage and sauerkraut
    (means "Alsace style")

amande, almond

amande de mer, small shellfish

amandine, w/almonds

amer/amère, bitter

américaine, white wine sauce usually w/brandy,
    shallots, tomatoes and garlic w/shrimp/lobster

Amer Picon, aperitif (wine and brandy w/herbs)

amidon, starch. *Amidon de blé* is cornstarch

amourettes, the bone marrow of an ox or calf

amuse-bouche, appetizer

amuse-gueule, appetizer

ananas, pineapple

anchoïade, anchovy spread from Provence

anchois, anchovy

ancienne, "old style": usually means a
    wine cream sauce w/mushrooms,
    shallots or onions

andalouse, usually w/eggplant, tomatoes
    and green peppers

[handwritten margin notes:]

Alouettes Sans têtes ~ Larks without heads!

Bouche ~ mouth
gueule ~ throat
These are small morsels of food. Just a mouthful or two.

andouille, tripe sausage
andouillette, small tripe sausage
aneth, dill
angélique, the crystallized stalks of
    the herb angelica
    (a decoration for cakes)
anglaise, boiled/boiled or steamed
    vegetables/breaded, fried meat,
    fish or vegetables

We have a general rule about tripe: Don't. But we love andouillette.

anguille, eel. Many dishes in the French West Indies feature eels
anguille au vert, eel in a white sauce w/parsley
anis, aniseed
apéritif, drink before dinner
à point, medium rare
appellation d'origine contrôlée, an officially recognized wine
    of France. Sometimes designated by A.O.C. The makers of
    A.O.C. are the best of the French wine industry
arachide, peanut
araignée de mer, spider crab
ardennaise, usually means served w/berries ("Ardennes style")
ardoise, specials are often written on the *ardoise*, a chalk board.
    This can also mean (for regular customers) that they put it
    on your running bill
arête, fish bone
argenteuil, asparagus soup
arlequin, two flavors
armagnac, brandy (similar to *cognac*). The main difference is
    cognac is distilled twice (and thus smoother)
    while *armagnac* is distilled only once
armoricaine, in a tomato sauce
arôme, aroma
aromates, herbs and spices
aromatisé, flavored
artichaut, artichoke
artichauts à la barigoule, artichokes w/mushrooms and pork
artichaut violet, small artichoke
asperge, asparagus
asperge à la flamande, white asparagus w/egg sauce.
    A Belgian specialty
asperge d'Argenteuil, large white artichoke
aspic, gelatin

aspic de volaille, chicken in aspic
assaisonnement, dressing/seasoning
assiette, plate
assiette anglaise, cold cuts
assiette de charcuterie, assorted meat products (cold cuts)
assiette de crudités, a plate of raw vegetables
assiette du pêcheur, assorted fish plate
assorti, assorted
asturienne, w/livers
au, in
aubergine, eggplant
aulx, garlic (the plural of *ail*)
aumônière, *crêpe* filled and wrapped into the shape of a little
    purse. The word means "beggar's purse"
aurore, a tomato sauce
auvergnat, usually means served w/sausage and cabbage (means
    "Auvergne style")
aux, with
avec, with
avec des glaçons, on the rocks
avocat, avocado
avoine, oats
aziminu, Corsican *bouillabaisse*
baba au rhum, spongecake soaked in rum
bäckaoffa, meat and potato stew from Alsace
bacon, Canadian bacon
baeckeoffe, baked meat and
    potato stew from Alsace
bagna cauda, hot anchovy dip from Provence
baguette, long and thin loaf of bread
baies, berries
baigné, bathed
ballottine (de volaille), boned meat
    (poultry) stuffed, rolled,
    cooked and served in gelatin
banane, banana
bananes flambées, bananas flamed in brandy
bananes vertes, green bananas used in dishes in the
    French West Indies
Bandol, popular wine from Provence. The red is full-bodied
    and spicy and the white is fruity, often with a hint of aniseed

Handwritten margin notes: "Aubergine." with a sketch of an eggplant; "Avec des glaçons." with a sketch of a glass; "Ballotine. Not sure about this concept."

banon, cheese from Provence dipped in *eau-de-vie* and wrapped in chestnut leaves

bar, bass

barbarie, Barbary (a type of duck)

barbouiado, vegetable *ragoût*

barbue, brill (fish)

barde, the lard or bacon put over roasts

barigoule, artichoke hearts, sausage, bacon, garlic and mushroom dish

Barigoule.
Like the sound of it

baron, the hindquarter and leg of a lamb

barquette, small boat-shaped pastry. *Une barquette* means "a carton of"

Barry, à la du, served w/a cauliflower and cheese sauce

basilic, basil

basquaise, served w/tomatoes, or red peppers ("Basque style")

bâtard, a small *baguette*

batonnets, crisp sticks. *Batonnets de courgette* are crisp zucchini sticks

baudroie, monkfish
This can also refer to a fish soup w/garlic and vegetables

bavaroise, custard dessert

bavette, flank steak

béarnaise, *hollandaise* sauce w/vinegar, tarragon, shallots and wine

Sauce Bearnais

béatilles, mixed organ meats

beaufort, a hard cheese

Beaujolais, one of France's wine regions (on the south tip of Burgundy) noted for fruity red wines. *Beaujolais Nouveau* is light and fruity and denotes the first wine to be released

beaumont, a mild cheese

bécasse, woodcock

bécassine, snipe

béchamel, white sauce (usually butter, milk [and/or cream] and flour)

beckenoff, pork and mutton baked w/potatoes

beignet, fritter filled w/fruit, meat and/or vegetables (a filled doughnut)

belle étoile, a mild cheese

belon, a type of oyster

bénédictine, dark green, brandy-based liqueur

Belle étoile ~ beautiful star.

bergamotte, a variety of lemon or pear

bercy, fish stock *velouté* w/white wine, shallots and parsley

berlingots, mint-flavored caramels

betterave, beet

beuchelle, creamed kidneys and sweetbreads

Betterave.

beurgoule, caramel-rice pudding

beurre, butter

beurre blanc, white butter sauce of white wine, vinegar and shallots

beurre blanc nantais, white butter and shallot sauce for fish

beurre d'ail, garlic butter

beurre d'anchois, anchovy butter

beurre de montpellier, green butter (made green from herbs)

beurre d'estragon, tarragon butter

beurre fondu, melted butter

beurre maître d'hôtel, butter w/chopped parsley and lemon juice

beurre manié, butter and flour thickening for sauces

beurre nantais, white butter

beurre noir, browned butter sauce (until it's almost black)

beurre noisette, lightly browned butter

bicard de soude, baking soda

biche, female deer

bien cuit, well done

bière, beer

bière à la pression, draft beer

bière blonde, lager beer

Bière.

bière brune, dark beer

bière légère, light beer

bifteck, beef steak

biftek de cheval, horse-meat steak

bigarade, brown sauce usually w/vinegar, sugar and oranges

bigarreau, a type of cherry

bigorneaux, small sea mollusks

bigourneau, the shellfish periwinkle

billes de melons, melon balls

billy bi, cream of mushroom soup

biscotte, zwieback (sweetened bread enriched w/eggs, baked and sliced and toasted until dry and crisp)

biscuit, biscuit/cookie
biscuit à la cuillère, ladyfingers
biscuit de Savoie, spongecake
biscuits aux brisures de chocolat,
    chocolate-chip cookies
bisque, chowder
bisque d'écrevisses, freshwater
    crayfish chowder
bisque de homard, lobster bisque
bisque de langoustines, saltwater
    crayfish chowder
blaff, spicy stewed fresh fish
    dish served in the
    French West Indies
blanc, white
blanc-cassis, white wine and
    black currant liqueur

*Bisque de...
ecrevisses, homard,
Langoustines...
Love 'em all.*

blanc de blancs, white wine made from white grapes
blanc de poireau, the white part of a leek
blanc de volaille, boned breast of poultry
blanchaille, whitebait, a fish
blanchi, blanched
blanquette, stew
blanquette de veau, veal
    stew in a white sauce
blé, wheat
blé de turquie, corn
blé dur, duram wheat
blette, Swiss chard

*Blanc Cassis
is a popular
aperatif
in France.*

bleu, blue cheese/meat prepared nearly raw/fish boiled very
    fresh. Some popular blue cheeses
    are bleu d'Auvergne, bleu de Bresse,
    bleu des Causses and bleu du Haut-Jura
blini, small pancakes (usually w/sour
    cream, caviar and salmon)
blonde, light (as in light-colored
    [lager] beer)
boeuf, beef

*In Canada
Blonde means
girl friend
no matter wha
color her hair.*

boeuf à la ficelle, beef cooked in stock
boeuf à la gardiane, beef and wine stew w/black olives
boeuf à la gordienne, braised beef dish from Provence

boeuf à la mode, beef marinated in red wine

boeuf bourguignon, beef stewed in red wine (burgundy) w/onions, bacon and mushrooms

boeuf braisé à la beauceronne, beef casserole found around Orléans

boeuf en daube, larded chunks of beef marinated and cooked in wine/beef casserole

boeuf miroton, beef stew or boiled beef w/onion sauce

boeuf mode, beef stew w/carrots. This can also refer to cold beef in jelly

boeuf salé, corned beef

bohémienne, eggplant and tomato casserole. A specialty in Nice

boisson, beverage

boissons compris, drinks included

boissons non compris, drinks not included

boîte, can, box or jar. *Une boîte de conserve...* means a can of...

boles de picolat, meatballs and mushrooms cooked in a sauce

bolet, boletus mushroom

bombe/bombe glacée, layered ice cream

bon, bonne, good

bonbons, candy

bonne femme, homestyle cooking. This can also refer to a *sauce veloutée* w/*crème fraîche* and lemon juice

Bonne femme means Good Woman.

bonnefoy, *sauce velouté* w/shallots and white wine

Bordeaux, one of France's wine regions (the largest wine-producing area in the world). Red *Bordeaux* is made from a blend of cabernet sauvignon, merlot, cabernet franc, malbec and petite verdot grapes. White *Bordeaux* is made from semillon and sauvignon blanc grapes.

bordelaise, red wine sauce w/mushrooms, beef marrow and shallots

botte, bunch (as in a bunch of herbs). *Botte de radis* means bunch of radishes

bouchée, bite size. *Cidre bouché* refers to alcoholic, dry cider

bouchée à la reine, puff pastry filled w/meat, seafood, sweet breads and/or mushrooms

boucherie, butcher shop. *Boucheries chevalines* are still found in France and are horse-meat butcher shops

bouchon, cork

boudin, blood sausage (black pudding)

boudin blanc, white sausage
(sausage of white meats)

boudin liège, Belgian sausage

boudin noir (boudin antillais), spicy
blood sausage (a specialty
in the French West Indies)

bougon, a goat's milk cheese

bouillabaisse, shellfish and fish stewed
in white wine, olive oil, saffron,
tomatoes and garlic. There are many versions of this dish

bouilli, boiled/boiled beef

bouillon, broth/stock

boulanger, baker. *Boulangère* is a woman baker

boulangerie, bakery

boule de fromage frit, fried cheese ball

boulette, meatball or fishball

boulette de semoule, semolina and potato *gnocchi*

boulghour, bulgur wheat

boullinade, thick soup found in the South of France

bouquet, large (red) shrimp (usually served cold)

bouquet garni, a small bundle of herbs
and/or spices tied together in
cheesecloth and used to provide
flavor to dishes while they cook

bouquet rose, prawns

bourbon, bourbon

bourboulhade, salt cod and garlic soup.
Sometimes referred to as
a poor man's *bouillabaisse*

bourdaines, apples baked in pastry

bourdaloue, butter cake w/fruit

Bourgogne, Burgundy. Burgundy is one of France's wine
regions (famous for red wines made from pinot noir grapes)

Bourgueil, light, fruity wine from the Loire Valley

bourguignon/bourguignonne, mushrooms and onions in a red
wine sauce (see *boeuf bourguignon*)

bouribut, red wine duck stew

bourride, a fish stew found in the South of France (thickened
w/egg yolks and *aïoli*)

boursin, a mild, soft cheese

boutargue, smoked fish roe

Boudin is also an unflattering term for a woman.

Bouquet garni can be found in boxes. Packaged like tea bags and are great.

60

bouteille, bottle
braisé, braised
braiser, to braise
branches de céleri, celery stalks
brandade, cod and potato dish
brandade de morue, salt cod w/garlic,
   cream and olive oil
brandy, brandy
brebis, sheep's-milk cheese
brème, bream
Bretagne, Brittany, an Atlantic coastal province
bretonne, usually a dish served w/white wine sauce or white
   beans ("Brittany style"). This can also refer to a type of
   oyster
brézzolles, slices of veal
bricks, round, paper-thin sheets of pastry (usually filled w/egg
   and Middle Eastern spices). A specialty of Tunisia
brie, white, mellow, soft cheese. If you don't know what *brie* is,
   you shouldn't be in France
brins, branches or sprigs
brioche, small sweet cake or roll
broccio, a cheese (similar to *ricotta*) found in Corsica
broche, (on a) spit
brochet, pike
brochette de coeurs, heart kabob. A specialty in Toulouse
brochette, en, cooked on a skewer
brocoli, broccoli
broufado, braised beef w/anchovies
brouillade d'aubergines, stuffed eggplant w/tomatoes
brouillé, scrambled
Brouilly, red wine from Beaujolais
brousse de brebis, soft and mild sheep's- or goat's-milk cheese
brousse du Rove, cheese (similar to *ricotta*) made w/sheep's
   milk. The sheep graze on
   thyme, which gives the cheese
   its unusual flavor
brugnon, nectarine
brûlé, burned/caramelized
brune, dark (as in dark beer)
brunoise, diced vegetables
brut, very dry

Bouteille ~ Bootay

Brins de romarin.

Brugnon.

bûche de Noël, rolled Christmas cake
buffet froid, a variety of cold dishes
bugnes, fried doughnuts
buisson, vegetable dish
bulot, large sea snail

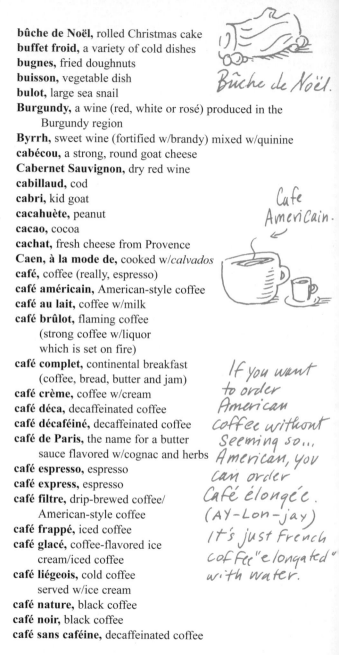

Bûche de Noël.

Burgundy, a wine (red, white or rosé) produced in the
    Burgundy region
Byrrh, sweet wine (fortified w/brandy) mixed w/quinine
cabécou, a strong, round goat cheese
Cabernet Sauvignon, dry red wine
cabillaud, cod
cabri, kid goat
cacahuète, peanut
cacao, cocoa
cachat, fresh cheese from Provence
Caen, à la mode de, cooked w/*calvados*
café, coffee (really, espresso)
café américain, American-style coffee
café au lait, coffee w/milk
café brûlot, flaming coffee
    (strong coffee w/liquor
    which is set on fire)
café complet, continental breakfast
    (coffee, bread, butter and jam)
café crème, coffee w/cream
café déca, decaffeinated coffee
café décaféiné, decaffeinated coffee
café de Paris, the name for a butter
    sauce flavored w/cognac and herbs
café espresso, espresso
café express, espresso
café filtre, drip-brewed coffee/
    American-style coffee
café frappé, iced coffee
café glacé, coffee-flavored ice
    cream/iced coffee
café liégeois, cold coffee
    served w/ice cream
café nature, black coffee
café noir, black coffee
café sans caféine, decaffeinated coffee

*Cafe
Americain.*

*If you want
to order
American
Coffee without
seeming so...
American, you
can order
Café élongée.
(AY-Lon-jay)
It's just French
coffee "elongated"
with water.*

café soluble, instant coffee
café viennois, coffee w/whipped cream
cagouille, small land snail
caille, quail
caillete, pâté of pork, herbs and garlic
calalou, "pepperpot" stew w/many
 ingredients found in the French West Indies
calamar, squid
calissons, marzipan candies
 shaped like boats from Aix
calmar, squid
calvados, apple brandy
camembert, soft cheese w/strong flavor
camomille, camomile tea
campagne, à la, this term means "country style" and has many
 different meanings
canapé, appetizer w/bread base and topped w/various ingredients
canard, duck
canard à la presse, roast duck dish w/red wine and Cognac
canard à l'orange, roast duck braised w/orange sauce
canard de Barbarie, a duck breed in Southwest France
canard de Challans, a type of small duck
canard de Nantes, a type of small duck
canard de Rouen, a type of wild duck
canard laqué, Peking duck
canard Montmorency, duck w/cherries
canard rôti, roast duck
canard sauvage, wild duck
cancoillotte, strong, hard cheese (melted before serving) from
 the Franche-Comté region in Eastern France
candi, candied
caneton, duckling
canette, young female duck
canistrelli, dry cookies from Corsica
cannelle, cinnamon
cantal, a cheese very much like cheddar
caouanne, turtle
capoun fassum, cabbage stuffed w/rice and sausage
câpre, caper
caqhuse, pork and onion casserole
carafe, carafe

Calmar.

Canard.

caramélisé, caramelized

caramel, burned sugar. This also refers to a
chewy vanilla or chocolate caramel

carapaces, shells

carbonnade, braised beef stew
(a Belgian specialty)
also charcoal-grilled meat

carbonnade à la boeuf, Belgian specialty of beef marinated in
beer and cooked in onions and herbs

carbonnade bruxelloise, Belgian dish of pork w/a tomato and
tarragon sauce

carbonnade flamande, beef, herbs and onions braised in beer

carbonnade nîmoise, lamb and potato dish

cardinal, fish stock *velouté*, lobster, butter and cream

cardamome, cardamom

cardon, cardoon (a member of the thistle family)

cargolade, grilled snail dish from
Languedoc-Roussillon

cari, curry

carotte, carrot

carottes glacées, carrots glazed in butter

carottes râpées, grated carrots

carottes Vichy, steamed carrots (in butter and parsley)

carpe, carp

carré, rack/loin/fillet

carré d'agneau, rack or loin of lamb

carré de l'Est, pungent cheese (square shaped)

carré de porc, rack or loin of pork

carré de veau, rack or loin of veal

carrelet, flounder/plaice

carte, la, menu

carte des vins, wine list

carvi, caraway seeds

casse-croûte, snack
("breaking the crust")

casse-pierre, seaweed

cassis, black currant/black currant liqueur

cassolette, dish served in a small casserole

cassoulet (toulousain), meat and bean (and often sausage)
casserole. This dish originated in Southwest France

castagna, chestnut in Corsican

[handwritten note:] Carapaces refers to shrimp or Lobster Shells.

[handwritten note:] The French are not so much for snacking, Casse-croute refers to a small-meal type snack.

castanhet, chestnut cake

cavaillon, a fragrant melon from the town of the same name in Provence. It looks like a small cantaloupe

cave, wine shop/wine cellar

caviar, fish eggs

caviar d'aubergine, eggplant purée

cédrat, citron

céleri, celery

Celeri.

céleri-rave, celery root

céleri rémoulade, celery root in a creamy mayonnaise dressing

cendre chemisée, smoldering

cèpe, boletus mushroom

céréale, cereal

cerf, venison (deer)

cerfeuil, chervil

cerise, cherry

cerise noire, black cherry

Cerf.

cerises jubilé, cherries flamed w/*kirsch* and served w/ice cream

cerneau, the "meat" of a walnut

cervelas, seasoned sausage made from brains

cervelle, brains

cervelle de canut, herbed cheese spread

Cervelle.
Apparently
some people
like it!

chabichou, cow's- and goat's-milk cheese. Some think it has a sweet flavor

Chablis, one of France's wine regions producing white wine made from the chardonnay grape

chair, "fleshy" part of fish or meat

Challonaise, wine region producing mostly table wine

chambré, room temperature (when serving wine)

chamois, mountain goat

Champagne, A region in Northeastern France famous for its sparkling wines classified by the sugar content. *Brut* is the driest, *extra-sec* is very dry, *sec* is dry, *demi-sec* is slightly sweet and *doux* is sweet. Also a sweet cookie served w/champagne

champenoise, sparkling wine

champêtre, this term means "rustic" and can mean many things – usually it signifies a simple dish

Champignons.

champignon, mushroom

champignon à la grecque, cold mushroom appetizer

champignon de bois, wild mushroom
champignon de Paris, button mushroom
champignon de pin, pine mushroom.
   A wild mushroom found in Provence
champignon sauvage, wild mushroom
changement de garniture, this means an extra charge for
   substitutions
chansons aux pommes, flaky breakfast
   pastry w/apple filling
chanterelle, chanterelle mushroom
chantilly, sweet whipped cream.
   This can also refer to
   hollandaise sauce and whipped cream
chaource, cheese found in the Champagne region
chapelure, breadcrumbs
chapon, capon
chapon de mer, scorpion fish
charbonnade, charcoal-grilled meat
charcuterie, can be a deli or any
   place serving prepared meats and salads.
   This can also refer to cooked pork meats/cold cuts
charcuterie assortie, assorted cold meats
chariot, dessert and/or cheese cart
charlotte, fruit dessert made in a
   mold/baked fruit compote/pudding
charolais, denotes a high-quality beef
chartreuse, yellow (or green) herb liqueur. Also a game bird
   (usually pheasant or partridge) dish from Alsace
chasse, venison
chasselas, a white grape
chasseur, "hunter's style" usually means
   in a sauce w/tomatoes,
   wine, herbs and mushrooms
châtaigne, chestnut
châtaignes chaudes/marrons chauds, roasted chestnuts
chateaubriand, thick slice of tenderloin stuffed w/sauteed
   shallots and usually served
   w/butter or *béarnaise* sauce
Château-Margaux, red wine from Bordeaux
Châteauneuf-du-Pape, red wine from
   the Rhône River valley

Chansons au pommes means Song to apples.

Chariot... be on the Lookout!

Chasse means hunt

Château neuf du Pape means the Pope's new castle.

chaud, hot

chaud-froid, cold poultry dish/a dish containing gelatin. It's cooked and then served cold, thus the name which means "hot-cold"

chaudrée, seafood and fish stew (contains the white part of squid)

chauffé, heated

chaumes, rich, creamy cheese from Dordogne

chausson, fruit turnover

chausson aux pommes, apple turnover

chemise, en, baked in parchment/wrapped in pastry/potato w/the skin left on

cheval, horse

chèvre, goat/goat cheese

chevreau, young goat

chèvre fraîche, goat cheese which is only a few days old

chèvre sèche, dried (aged) goat cheese

chevreuil, deer

chichi, orange-flavored doughnuts/can also mean "fancy"

chicons du Nord, Belgian endive

chicorée, chicory/endive

chicorée frisée, curly lettuce

chicorée witloof, Belgian endive

chiffonnade, shredded leafy vegetables and herbs

chinchard, saurel, a fish

chinois, Chinese

Chinon, red wine from the Loire Valley

chipiron, small squid

chipirons en su tinta, Basque dish of squid cooked in its own ink

chipolatas, small sausages

chips, potato chips

chivry, a *béarnaise* sauce w/spinach, parsley or watercress added to make it green

chocolat, chocolate

chocolat à la bayonne, chocolate cream dessert

chocolat amer, bitter chocolate

chocolat au lait, milk chocolate

chocolat chaud, hot chocolate

chocolat mi-amer, bittersweet chocolate

Hot Chocolate is more common in Europe than in the U.S.

67

chocolat noir, bitter chocolate/black chocolate

choix, "choice." On a menu, this means you can choose among a list of dishes

chope, large beer

choron, *béarnaise* sauce w/tomatoes

chou, cabbage

chou à la crème, cream puff

choucroute, sauerkraut. In Alsace, this refers to a dish of cabbage w/pork, potatoes and sauerkraut

Love choucroute garni !

choucroute garnie, sauerkraut w/ham, pork sausage or frankfurters

chouée, buttered cabbage dish

Mon petit chou is a term of endearment.

chou-fleur, cauliflower

chou frisé, kale/savoy cabbage

chou marin, kale

chou rouge, red cabbage

chou vert, green cabbage

choux de Bruxelles, brussels sprouts

ciboule, scallion

ciboulette, chive

cidre, cider. Popular in Brittany

cigales, a type of clam

cigarette, sugar cookie (rolled in the shape of a cigarette)

citron, the term for lemons-and limes (citrus fruit) but can also simply refer to a lemon

citronelle, lemon grass

citronnade, lemon drink

citron pressé, fresh lemon juice w/sugar and water (lemonade)

citron vert, lime

citrouille, pumpkin

civelles, baby eels

civet, game stew. Popular in Corsica

civet de lapin, rabbit stew

civet de lièvre, hare stew

clafouti, fruit baked in pancake batter *LOVE this*

clafouti du limousin, cherry *clafouti*

claires, oysters (raised in an oyster bed)

clamart, stuffed w/green peas

Claret, dry, red table wine from Bordeaux

clémentine, seedless tangerine

clos, vineyard

clou de girofle, clove

clouté, "studded with"

cocaos, cocoa

cochon, pig

cochon de lait, suckling pig *Cochon.*

cochon de lait en gelée, suckling pig in aspic *I'll pass.*

cochonnailles, assorted pork sausages and pâtés

cocotte, casserole *Cocotte.*

coeur, heart

coeur d'artichaut, artichoke heart

coeur de filet, thickest and best part of a beef filet

coeurs de palmiers, hearts of palm served w/a mustard vinaigrette

cognac, cognac

coing, quince

Cointreau, orange-flavored liqueur

colbert, à la, dipped in batter and breadcrumbs and fried

colin, hake

colonel, lemon sherbet w/vodka

colvert, wild duck

complet, full/whole

compote, stewed fruit

compote de..., stewed

compris, included

comté, a mild cheese (similar to the Swiss gruyère cheese)

concassé, chopped

concentré, concentrate

concombre, cucumber

concorde, chocolate meringue and chocolate mousse

condiments, seasoning

confiserie, candy and sweets shop

confit, goose, pork, turkey or duck preserved in fat.
   Also vegetables/fruit preserved in alcohol, sugar or vinegar

confiture, jam/preserves.
   Confiture d'oignons is onion compote

confiture de vieux garçon, fruit served in alcohol

confiture d' orange, marmalade

congre, conger eel

consommation, drinks

consommé, broth (clear soup)

Vieux Garçon means Old boy. Something like old maid.

consommé aux vermicelles, broth w/thin noodles
consommé Célestine, broth w/chicken and noodles
consommé colbert, broth w/vegetables and poached eggs
consommé madrilène, cold broth w/tomatoes
consommé princesse, broth w/chicken and asparagus
consultez aussi l'ardoise, other suggestions
    on the blackboard
consultez notre carte des desserts, consult our dessert menu
contre-filet, sirloin
copeaux, shavings (of vegetables or chocolate)
copieux, filling
coppa, fillet (in Corsica)
coq, rooster
coq au vin, chicken stewed in red wine
    w/bacon, onions, mushrooms and herbs
coq de bruyère, grouse
coque, tiny shellfish (similar to a clam)
coquelet, cockerel
coquillage, shellfish
coquille, shell/scallop
coquille Saint-Jacques, scallops (prepared w/a
    parsley butter or a cream sauce)
coquilles à la nantaise, scallops w/onions.
    A specialty in Brittany
corail, the egg sac of lobster,
    crayfish or scallops
corbeille, basket
corbeille de fruits, basket of assorted fruits
cordon bleu, veal slices stuffed w/ham and
    gruyere, breaded and fried in butter
coriandre, coriander
cornet de frites, paper cone filled
    w/french fries. A popular snack
cornets de murat, cones filled w/cream
cornichon, small pickle (gherkin)
corniottes, cheese pastries made in the shape of hats
corps, refers to the "body" of wine
corsoise, à la, this means that the dish is prepared
    as it would be in Corsica
cosse, pod/husk
côte, rib/chop

Coq au vin
gotta have
it in
Paris

Coquille.

Corbeille.

côte d'agneau, lamb chop
Côte de Beaune, red and white wines from Beaune in Burgundy
côte de boeuf, beef rib steak/T-bone steak
Côte de Nuits, a heavy red Burgundy wine
côte de veau, veal chop
côtelette, cutlet/chop
côtelette d'agneau, lamb chop
côtelette de porc, pork chop
Côtes du Rhône, wine region producing wines such as
    Châteauneuf-du-Pape, Côte-Rotie, Hermitage and *Tavel*
côtes levées, spareribs
cotignac, caramelized apple tart
cotriade, fish stew (from Brittany)
cou, neck
cou d'oie farci, a "sausage" made of the neck skin of a goose
    which is stuffed w/meat and spices
couennes de porc, fresh pork rinds
coulibiac, salmon *pâté*
coulis, vegetable, shellfish or fruit purée
coulis de tomates, thick tomato sauce
coulommiers, a mild cheese (similar to *brie*)
coupe, goblet/scoop/a dish used for serving dessert
coupe Danemark, a scoop of vanilla ice
    cream covered w/hot chocolate sauce
coupe de champagne, a flute of champagne
coupe des îles, a scoop of vanilla ice cream
    w/fruit and whipped cream

Coupe de Champagne.

coupe glacée, ice cream dessert (often a sundae)
courge, squash
courgette, zucchini
courgettes au broccio, *broccio* cheese-stuffed
    zucchini dish from Corsica
couronne, circle-shaped or ring-shaped bread
court bouillon, seafood broth

Couronne means crown or wreath.

couscous, Moroccan specialty of steamed grain, broth, meats,
    vegetables and other ingredients
couscous royal, *couscous* w/meat
cousinat, bean, bell pepper, artichoke, tomato, green onion and
    carrot dish
couteau, knife

Couteau - coo·toe.

couvert, cover charge/place setting

couvert, vin et service compris, the price includes wine, tip and cover charge

crabe, crab

crabe verte, shore crab

crapaudine, grilled game or poultry dish

craquelins, cookies

Crécy, à la, served w/carrots

crème, cream/creamy soup/creamy dessert. Can also refer to sweet liqueur as in *crème de menthe*. *À la crème* means served w/a cream sauce

crème à la vanille, vanilla custard

crème allégée, light cream

crème anglaise, custard

crème brûlée, custard dessert topped w/caramelized sugar

crème caramel, vanilla custard w/caramel sauce

crème catalane, caramel-covered trifle w/cinnamon and anise

crème champignons, cream of mushroom soup

crème chantilly, vanilla-flavored and sweetened whipped cream

crème d'asperges, cream of asparagus soup

crème de cacao, cocoa-flavored liqueur

crème de cassis, black currant liqueur

crème de marrons, chestnut purée

crème de menthe, mint-flavored liqueur

crème de poireaux, cream of leek soup

crème de poulet, cream of chicken soup

crème de volaille, cream of chicken soup

crème épaisse, heavy cream

crème fouettée, whipped cream

crème fraîche, thick, heavy cream

crème frit, fried cream custard dessert from Burgundy

crème glacée, ice cream

crème pâtissière, custard filling in cakes and pastry

crème plombières, custard filled w/fresh fruit

crème renversée, custard dessert in a mold

crèmerie, store selling dairy products

cremets, cream made in molds w/fruit

crêpe, crepe (thin pancake). Popular in Brittany

crêpe froment, buckwheat crepe w/sweet filling

crêpe Suzette, crepe w/orange sauce, flamed w/orange liqueur

crépine, caul fat (fat covering the intestines) used to wrap *pâtés* and *terrines*

[handwritten note: We like anything with crème attached.]

crépinette, small sausage patty wrapped in caul fat

cresson, watercress

cressonade, watercress sauce

cressonière, watercress soup

crête de coq, cock's comb
    (the fleshy crest on the head of fowl)

YES, they eat this.

creuse, a type of oyster

crevette, shrimp

crevette grise, gray, small shrimp

crevette rose, red shrimp w/firm flesh

cristallisés, crystallized

crist-marine, algae

croissant, crescent-shaped flaky breakfast
    roll made of flour, eggs and butter

croquant, crispy

croquants, crispy honey or almond cookies

croque madame, toasted ham and
    cheese sandwich topped w/an egg

croquembouche, cream-puff tree

Croquembouche. Typically served at weddings.

croque monsieur, toasted ham
    and cheese sandwich

croquette, ground meat, fish or vegetables
    coated in bread crumbs and deep fried

crosse, shank

crottin/croutin de chavignol, a firm
    goat cheese

croustade, pie filled w/meat, seafood and/or vegetables

croustillant, crisp/spicy

croûte, crust   *Yes, please.*

croûte au fromage, melted cheese served on a slice of toast

croûte de sel, en, in a salt crust

croûte, en, in a pastry crust

croûte forestière, mushrooms on toast

croûtes, croutons

croûton, small toasted piece of bread, usually served in a salad

cru, raw. On a wine list, this means vintage

cru classé, high-quality wine

crudités, raw vegetables

crustacé, shellfish (crustaceans)   *Cuiller ~ Qui-air*

cuiller, spoon

cuillère, à la, a dish eaten w/a spoon

73

cuisine, there are four categories of French cuisine:

> *Cuisine campagnarde* (also known as
> > *cuisine des provinces*):
> > Traditional regional dishes prepared
> > with fresh ingredients.
>
> *Cuisine bourgeoise*: French home cooking.
> *Haute cuisine*: An elaborate meal with many
> > courses featuring
> > rich and fresh ingredients.
>
> *Nouvelle cuisine*: Light sauces and small portions that
> > emphasize the colors and textures of the ingredients.

cuisse, leg and thigh (denotes dark meat)

cuisse de poulet, chicken drumstick w/thigh

cuisses de grenouilles, frogs' legs

cuissot, haunch of game or veal

cuit, cooked

cuit à la vapeur, steamed

cuit au four, baked

cul, haunch

cul de veau, veal pot roast

culotte, rump

cumin, cumin

curaçao, orange-flavored liqueur

curcuma, the spice turmeric (used in curry powder)

cure-dent, (served w/a) toothpick

currie/curry, curry

cuvée, blend of wines or champagne/house wine

Cynar, aperitif w/an artichoke base

darne, thick fillet of fish (often salmon)

dartois, pastry w/jam

datte, date

daube, stew

daube à la niçoise, beef or lamb stew w/red wine,
tomatoes and onions

daube de boeuf, beef stew

daube provençal, gravy w/capers, garlic and anchovies

dauphinois, a mild cheese

daurade, white fish (usually served grilled) found in the South
of France (sea bream)

déca, decaf

décafféiné, decaffeinated

[handwritten margin notes: Cuisse ~ Kweece is dark meat; déca ~ day-cah]

décortiqué, shelled/peeled

déglacée, warmed up

dégustation, sampling/tasting

déjeuner, lunch

délice, a delight/a treat

délimité de qualité supérieure, on a wine bottle, this means a superior-quality wine

demi, half/small beer

demi-bouteille, half bottle

demi-deuil, usually means served w/truffles

demidoff, w/vegetables

demi-glace, beef-stock sauce

demi-sel, soft, salty cream cheese/salted butter

demi-sec, medium dry

demoiselle de Cherbourg, small lobster

denté, dentex (fish)

désossé, boned

dessert, dessert

diable, hot, spicy sauce (often, a strong mustard sauce)/ devilled.) This is also the term for an unglazed, porous pot used to cook vegetables

diabolo, a drink usually mixed w/lemonade

diane, a brown sauce w/vinegar and peppercorns

dieppoise, shrimp and mussels served in a white wine sauce

digestif, after-dinner drink

dijonnaise, served w/mustard

dinde, turkey

dindon, turkey

dindonneau, young turkey

dîner, dinner

diplomate, custard dessert w/spongecake, crystallized fruit and topped w/liqueur

discrétion, when you see this on a menu, it means that you can drink as much wine as you want (for a fixed price)

divine, *hollandaise* sauce w/sherry

dodine de canard, stuffed-duck dish

domaine, on a wine label this notes a high-quality wine

dorade, sea bream

[handwritten notes:]
demi-bouteille ~
deh-mee.
boo-tay

dinde ~ dand
dindon ~ dan-dong
dindonea ~ dandon-oh

doré(e), golden

dos, back

dos et ventre, both sides (means "back and front")

douce, sweet

doucette, salad green (a cousin of *mâche*)

douceurs, desserts

doux, mild, sweet

douzaine, dozen

dragées, candied almonds

Dubonnet, wine and brandy-based aperitif w/herbs

duchesse, potatoes mixed w/egg and forced through a pastry tube

dugléré, a white sauce w/tomatoes, shallots and white wine

duxelles, finely chopped sautéed mushrooms

eau, water

eau au syphon, w/seltzer water

eau avec gaz, carbonated water

eau de source, spring water

eau-de-vie, brandy made from
distilled fruit juice. Sold in
elaborate tall and thin bottles in Alsace. The term means
"water of life." This can also refer to any spirit

Don't worry you can drink the water in France.

eau du robinet, tap water

eau glacée, iced water

eau minérale, mineral water

eau minérale gazeuse, carbonated mineral water

eau nature, tap water

eau plate, still (not sparkling) water

eau sans gaz, water w/out carbonation

écailler, oyster opener/fish scaler

échalote, shallot

échine, spareribs

éclair, pastry filled w/vanilla custard and topped
w/chocolate icing

écrevisse, crayfish

écrevisse à la nage, crayfish
in a white wine sauce

édam français, nutty-flavored,
orange-colored cheese
originally from the Netherlands

Ecrevisse.

édulcorant, artificial sweetener

effilée, thinly sliced

effiloché, thinly sliced
églefin, haddock
emballé, wrapped
embeurré, buttered/buttery
embeurrée de chou, buttered cabbage
émincé, slices of cooked meat in gravy/anything thinly sliced
émincé de veau, sauteed veal slices w/creme sauce
emmental, Swiss cheese
emporter, à, take-out foods

Sounds good.
Never had it.

émulsionné, liquified
enchaud de porc à la périgourdine, pork loin stuffed ⟵
    w/truffles. A specialty in Southwest France
encornet, small squid
endive, endive/chicory
enrubanne, layered dish
    (looks like ribbons)

entier, whole
entrecôte, rib-eye steak

Endive.

entrecôte Bercy, steak w/wine sauce
entrecôte maître d'hôtel, rib-eye steak served w/herb butter
entrecôte marchand de vin, rib-eye steak served in
    red wine sauce
Entre-Deux-Mers, a region of Bordeaux
    that produces white wine
entrée, first course/appetizer
entremets, dessert
épaule, shoulder
épeautre, a variety of wheat

EPICERIE

éperlan, smelt
épice, spice
épicé, peppered/spicy
épicerie, small grocery store
épi de maïs, miniature corn
    on the cob (often pickled)

Be sure to visit
a grocery
store ~ small
or large,
they're worth
the trip.

épinard, spinach
épinards en branches, leaf spinach
époisse, a cow's-milk cheese from Burgundy
érable, maple
escabèche, raw fish marinated in lime juice and herbs. In
    Provence, this can refer to a cold marinated sardine dish
escalope, scallop/cutlet

escalope de veau, veal scallop
escalope panée, breaded veal scallop
escalope viennoise, breaded veal
    cutlet (weiner schnitzel)
escargot, snail
escargot de mer, sea snail
escargot petit-gris, small snail
escarole, a type of *endive*
espadon, swordfish

Escargot.

essence, essence
estocaficada, cod stew
estofat de boeuf, beef stew
estouffade, beef stew. Can also refer to a steamed dish
estouffados, almond butter cookies found in Provence
estragon, tarragon
esturgeon, sturgeon
et, and

Estragon.

étrille, small crab
étouffée, stewed
étuvé/étuvée, steamed
éventail, en, cut into a fan shape
express, espresso
extra-sec, very dry (champagne)
façon, in the manner of
faisan, pheasant

faisan

faisan normand, pheasant w/apples and *calvados*
faisselle, fresh cow's-milk cheese
fait à la maison, homemade
falette, stuffed breast of veal
far, prune tart
farandole, dessert and/or cheese cart
farce, spiced ground meat (usually pork) used for stuffing
farci, stuffed, as in ***chou farci*** (stuffed cabbage)
    and ***tomates farcies*** (stuffed tomatoes).
    In Nice, this is a dish of   ←   *Love these*
    stuffed vegetables
farigoule, the name in Provence for wild thyme
farine, flour
farine de blé, wheat flour
farine de maïs, corn flour
faux-filet, flank steak/sirloin steak

fécule, starch. *Fécule de pommes de terre* is potato flour used
    to thicken sauces and soups

fécule de maïs, cornstarch

fendant, "melting." Refers to extremely tender meat
    or chocolate

fenouil, fennel

féra, dace (lake salmon)

ferme, farm/farm fresh

fermier, poultry raised on a farm

feu de bois, cooked on a wood fire

feuille, leaf

feuille de chêne, oak-leaf lettuce

feuille de laurel, bay leaf

feuille de vigne, vine leaf

feuilles farcies, grape leaves stuffed w/rice and herbs

feuilletage, puff pastry

feuilletée, puff pastry

fève, broad bean

fiadone, cheesecake found in Corsica

ficelle, small baguette. *Ficellé* means tied w/a string

figatelli, Corsican liver sausage

figue, fig

figue de barbarie, prickly pear

filet, fillet

filet à la mistral, filet of sole w/tomatoes and mushrooms

filet de boeuf, beef fillet

filet de boeuf à la Poitou, beef fillet w/chicken liver *pâté*

filet de boeuf Bordelaise, beef fillet in a red wine sauce

filet de sole, fillet of sole

filet de sole meunière, fillet of sole fried in butter

filet doria, fillet of sole w/cucumbers

filet mignon, small round beef tenderloin fillet

filet Saint-Germain, fillet of sole w/potatoes

financière, cream and Madeira wine sauce. This can also refer to
    a dish w/veal or chicken dumplings

fine, a fine brandy

fines de claire, oysters

fines herbes, mixture of herbs (such as parsley, chives, tarragon
    and thyme)

flageolets, small kidney-shaped beans

flagnarde/flaugnarde, fruit-filled cake

[handwritten note: Feu de bois on a sign outside a restaurant indicates that they cook with wood.]

[handwritten note: ficelle means string.]

[handwritten note: figues.]

flamande, à la, "Flemish style" w/potatoes, stuffed cabbage
leaves, vegetables, sausage and bacon

flambé(e), flaming

flamiche, savory tart (similar to a quiche)

flan, tart or crustless pie. Can also refer to the caramel custard
dessert of the same name found in Spain

flanchet, flank

flet, flounder

flétan, halibut

fleur, flower. *Fleurs* are crystallized flowers used on desserts

fleurette, small flower

Fleurie, a red wine from Beaujolais

fleurons, crescent-shaped puff pastries

fleurs de courgettes farcies, zucchini flowers stuffed w/cheese

flocon, flake

flocons d'avoine, oat flakes

florentine, w/spinach

foie, liver

foie de veau, calf's liver

foie de veau grand-mère, sautéed calf's liver w/bacon,
onion and potato garnish

foie de volaille, chicken liver

foie gras, fattened goose liver

foie gras de canard, fattened duck liver

foie gras d'oie, fattened goose liver

foie gras en brioche, fattened goose liver that is marinated and
cooked and baked a second time in a pastry shell

foies blonds de volaille, chicken livers

foin, cooked in hay ⟵ *I'd rather not.*

fond, bottom

fondant, cake icing

fondant au chocolat, similar to a brownie (but better!)

fond d`artichaut, artichoke heart

fondu/fondue (au fromage), melted cheese in a pot. Dip your
bread or meat in!

fondu aux raisins, the crust of this smooth and creamy cheese is
made of grape pulp. Also known as *tomme au marc*

fondue bourguignonne, small pieces of meat dipped into
oil and eaten w/sauces

fondue chinoise, thin slices of beef dipped in bouillon
and eaten w/sauces

fondue savoyarde, pot of melted cheese for dipping
forestière, ("forester's style") usually means w/sautéed
    mushrooms
forêt noire, Black Forest cake
forme d'Ambert, a blue cheese
formule, une, a set-price menu
fort, strong (as in strong or sharp cheese)
fougasse, decorated bread loaf w/olive oil flavoring and
    sometimes w/bacon, onion or tomato stuffing
fougassette, a slice of *brioche* bread flavored
    w/orange and saffron
four, au, baked
fourchette, fork
fournée, baked
fournitures, fresh herbs and salad greens
fourré, filled/stuffed
fraîche, fresh   *Fraîche - fraysh*
frais, fresh   *Frais - fray*
fraise, strawberry   *Fraise - frez*
fraise des bois, wild strawberry
framboise, raspberry/raspberry liqueur
frangipane, almond custard filling
frappé, drink blended w/ice
frémis, oysters (served almost raw)
friand, meat-filled pastry
friandises, *petits fours*
fricadelles, fried meat patties
fricadelles à la bière, meatballs in beer. A specialty in Belgium
fricandeau, braised veal dish
fricassée, a stew of meat, poultry or fish finished w/cream
fricassée liégeoise, fried eggs, bacon and sausage. A specialty in
    Belgium
frigolet, name in Provence for wild thyme
frisée, curly endive
frit, fried
fritelli, chestnut-flour doughnuts from Corsica
frites, french fries (often eaten w/mayonnaise) *← yes!*
fritons, minced spread made of organ meats *← No!*
fritot, batter fried or fritter
friture, frying
friture de mer/friture de poisson, fried small fish

froid, cold

Froid ~ Fwa

fromage, cheese. It is said that
there are over 400 different French cheeses

fromage à pâte dure, hard cheese

fromage à pâte molle, soft cheese

fromage au marc, a sharp, tangy cheese

I don't think so.

fromage blanc, cream cheese (but runny)

fromage de brebis, sheep's-milk cheese

fromage de chèvre, goat's-milk cheese

fromage de tête, headcheese (sausage made from the meat of a
calf's or pig's head cooked in a gelatinous meat
broth and then served cold)

fromage fermier, cheese made where the milk is produced

fromage fort, extremely soft cheese from Provence mixed
w/herbs, salt, pepper and *marc*

fromage maigre, low-fat cheese

fromagerie, cheese shop

fruit, fruit

Fruit ~ fru-ee

fruit confit, candied fruit

fruit de la passion, passion fruit

fruits de mer, seafood

fumé, smoked

fumet, fish stock

galantine, cold gelatinized meat dish

galette, buckwheat pancake. *Galettes de blé de sarrasin* are
crêpes made w/dark flour and filled w/cheese, ham,
an egg, mushrooms or any number of things.
Galettes de blé de froment are dessert crêpes made with
light flour. *Galette* can also refer to a flaky pastry "cake"
w/an almond paste filling. This is the traditional cake served
on Three Kings' Day. A bean (now a little porcelain statue is
used) is put in the cake and the person who gets the piece
containing the bean is king or queen for the day and wears a
a gold crown

galette bretonne, butter and rum cake

galette de pommes, apple tart

galette de sarrasin, buckwheat pancake w/savoury filling
popular in Brittany

galopin, bread pancake

Gamay de Touraine, red wine made w/the Gamay grape

gambas, large prawns

gambas à la planxa, grilled shrimp served on a plank of wood

ganses, fried cakes topped w/sugar

garbure, cabbage soup. In Southern France, this is usually cabbage soup w/ham

garni(e), w/vegetables/garnished

garniture, vegetables/garnished

gâteau, cake

gâteau au chocolat, chocolate cake

gâteau au fromage, cheese tart

gâteau de Savoie, spongecake

gâteau de riz, rice pudding

gateau ~ gat-oh

gaufre, waffle. A specialty in Belgium

gaufrette, sweet wafer

gayettes, small sausage patties

gazeuse, carbonated.

   Non-gazeuse means not carbonated

gelé, frozen

gelée, jellied/in aspic

gélinotte, prairie chicken

genièvre, juniper berry

génoise, spongecake

germiny, sorrel and cream soup/w/sorrel

*Gelée. Hmmm.
not something
we eat with
gusto.*

gésier, gizzard

Gewürztraminer, dry white wine from Alsace

gibelotte de lapin, rabbit stew

gibier, game

gigot, leg

gigot d'agneau, leg of lamb

gigot de mer, oven-roasted monkfish dish

gigot de mouton pré-salé, leg of lamb dish made w/lambs that graze in salt meadows in Northwest France

gigot farci, stuffed leg of lamb

gigue, the haunch of game meat

gimblettes, ring cookies

gin, gin

gingembre, ginger

gin tonique, gin and tonic

girofle, clove

girolle, chanterelle mushroom

glaçage, frosting

glace, ice/ice cream

glacé, iced/glazed

glace à la napolitaine, layers of different-flavored ice cream

glace au fondant, shiny cake icing

glace crémeuse, ice cream

glace de viande, concentrated meat stock (meat glaze)

glace de poisson, concentrated fish stock

glaçons, ice

globe, round (cut of meat)

gnocchi, gnocchi (potato dumplings). Found frequently on menus in Nice and near the Italian border

gnocchi aux blettes, gnocchi w/Swiss chard incorporated into the dough

gougère, cheese-flavored pastry ← *Oui, s'il vous plaît.*

goujon, gudgeon (related to carp)

goujonnettes, small slices of fish

gourmandises, sweets/candies

gousse, clove

gousse d'ail, clove of garlic

goûter, snack/to taste

graine, grain/seed

graine de maïs, corn meal

graine de moutarde, mustard seed

graines de paradis, similar to the spice cardamom and found in the former French African colonies

graisse, fat

graisserons, fried pieces of goose or duck skin *Graisserons. These are like cracklings and used as garnish.*

grand, large

grand crème, a large milky coffee

grand cru, high-quality wine

Grand Marnier, orange liqueur

grand-mère, means "grandmother." A garnish usually of mushrooms, potatoes and bacon

grand veneur, brown sauce w/red currants (usually served w/game)

grand vin, high-quality wine

granité, slushy iced drink

gras, fat/fatty

gras-double, tripe simmered in wine and onions

gratin, au, topped w/grated cheese, breadcrumbs and butter and then baked

gratin dauphinois, potato au gratin dish w/eggs, cheese and cream

gratin de fruits de mer, shellfish in a cream sauce

gratin de queues d'écrevisses, freshwater crayfish served *au gratin*

gratin de capucins, *gratin* of stuffed artichoke hearts

gratin savoyard, baked sliced-potato casserole

gratiné, prepared w/breadcrumbs

gratinée, topped w/cheese/onion soup

grattons, fried pieces of pork, goose or duck skin

gratuit, free

Graves, wine region of Bordeaux

grecque, cold vegetable mixture (*légumes à la grecque*). *À la grecque* refers to dishes stewed in oil (in the Greek style)

grelot, small white onion

grenade, pomegranate

grenadin, small veal scallop

grenoblois, caramel-walnut cake

grenouille, frog

gribiche, mayonnaise w/gherkins and capers. *Sauce gribiche* can refer to a vinaigrette and egg sauce

grillade, grilled meat/mixed grill

grillé, grilled

griotte, a type of cherry (usually in white alcohol)

grive, thrush (a bird)

grondin, spiked-headed ocean fish (gurnet)

gros bout de poitrine, brisket

groseille, currant

groseille à maquereau, gooseberry/currant

groseille rouge, red currant

gros sel, coarse salt

grumes, heavy coating or skin

Gruyère

gruyère, Swiss cheese

guimauve, marshmallow

haché, hashed

hachis, hash

hachis parmentier, shepherd's pie (ground meat and mashed potatoes topped w/a white sauce and served in a casserole)

hareng, herring

harengs fumés à la Créole, spicy smoked herring dish flamed in rum (found in the French West Indies)

haricot, bean

haricot de mer, tiny clam

haricot de mouton, mutton, bean and potato stew

haricot de soisson, navy bean/kidney bean

haricot rouge, red kidney bean

haricots en salade, bean salad

haricots verts, green beans (french beans)

Henri IV, artichoke hearts and *béarnaise* sauce

herbes, herbs

herbes de Provence, mixture of herbs that includes fennel, lavender, marjoram, bay leaf, sage, rosemary and thyme

hérisson de mer, sea urchin

hochepot, oxtail stew *We like the name.*

hollandaise, sauce of melted butter, egg yolks and lemon juice

homard, lobster

homard à l'américaine, flaming lobster dish w/white wine, herbs, tomatoes and garlic

homard à l'armoricaine, lobster in a tomato sauce

homard cardinal, flaming lobster dish w/mushrooms and truffles

homard froid à la parisienne, cold lobster garnished w/diced vegetables in a mayonnaise sauce

homard Newburg, lobster cooked in a sauce made of butter, cream, wine (or brandy) and egg yolks

homard Thermidor, flaming lobster dish w/white wine, herbs, spices and mustard

hongroise, served w/paprika and cream (means "Hungarian")

hors-d'oeuvre, appetizer

huile, oil

huile d'arachide, peanut oil

huile de carthame, safflower oil

huile de noix, walnut oil

huile de soya, soybean oil

huile de tournesol, sunflower oil

huile d'olive (vierge), olive oil (virgin)

huître, oyster

huître belon, pink oyster

huître portugaise, Portuguese lobster (small and fat)

hure de porc, pig's head

Hors d'oeuvre. means without work.

hure de saumon, salmon pâté

hysope, the bitter herb hysop

île flottante, meringues floating in a cream sauce

impératrice, rice-pudding dessert

importée, imported

indienne, w/curry (in the style of India)

infusion, herbal tea

jalousies, apricot pastry

jambe, leg

jambon, ham

jambon à l'os, baked ham

jambon blanc, boned, cooked ham

jambon cuit, cooked ham

jambon cuit d'Ardennes, smoked ham found in Belgium

jambon de Bayonne, raw, salty ham

jambon de canard, cured, salted or smoked duck or goose breast

jambon de montagne, local cured ham

jambon de Paris, lightly salted ham

jambon de Parme, Parma ham (prosciutto)

jambon de pays, local "country" cured ham

jambon de York, smoked ham (English style)

jambon d'oie, cured, salted or smoked duck or goose breast

jambon cru, cured ham

jambonneau, pork knuckle

jambon persillé, parsleyed ham

jardinière, w/diced vegetables

jarret, shank/knuckle

jarret de veau, veal shank (usually a stew)

jerez, sherry (Spanish for sherry)

Jésus de Morteau, smoked pork sausage

jeune, young/green (as in unripe)

joue, cheek

jour, du, of the day

jud mat gardebóneh, smoked pork and bean dish found in Luxembourg

julienne, vegetables cut into fine strips. There is also a fish w/this name

jumeau, pot roast

[handwritten notes:]
île flottante... don't see the appeal of this but it's very popular.

à l'os means bone-in.

Never warmed up to this

87

Jura, one of France's wine-growing regions

jus, juice/gravy

jus de tomate, tomato juice

jus d'orange, orange juice

kaki, persimmon

kalouga, chocolate-pudding cake

ketchup, ketchup

kig-ha-farz, buckwheat pudding
w/vegetables and meat

kir, apéritif made w/*crème de cassis* and wine

kir royal, apéritif made w/champagne and *crème de cassis*

kirsch, cherry-flavored liqueur

kougelhopf/kouglof/kugelhopf, Alsatian cake w/raisins
and almonds

kouigh amann, buttered pastry

l', la, le, the (singular). *Les* is the (plural)

lait, milk

laitance, fish roe

lait de beurre, buttermilk

lait écrémé, skim milk

lait entier, whole milk

laitue, lettuce

lambi, conch found in the French West Indies

lamelle, very thin slice

lamproie, lamprey

langouste, crayfish

langouste à la sètoise, lobster (crawfish) w/garlic, tomatoes and
cognac

langoustine, prawn

langue, tongue

langue de chat, biscuit and ice-cream dessert

Languedoc, one of France's wine-growing regions

languedocienne, usually means eggplant,
tomato and mushroom garnish

lapereau, young rabbit

lapin, rabbit

lapin à l'artésienne, rabbit stew

lapin à la Lorraine, rabbit in a
mushroom and cream sauce

lapin aux pruneaux, rabbit w/prunes.
A popular dish in Northern France

Jus d'orange is usually served with water and sugar.

Lamproie — yikes.

Langue de chat means cat's tongue.

Lapin Sworn enemy of all gardeners.

lapin chasseur, rabbit in a white wine and herb sauce
lapin de garenne, wild rabbit
lapin en paquets, rabbit pieces in a packet
 of bacon. A specialty in Provence
lard, bacon
lardon, diced bacon
laurier, bay leaf

Laurier.

lavande, lavender. Lavender blossoms are added to dishes in
 Provence such as *sorbet de lavande* (lavender sorbet)
lèche, thin slice (usually of meat or bread)
léger, light
légère, light (as in light beer)
légumes, vegetables
lentilles, lentils
levraut, young rabbit
levure, yeast
libre service, self-service
lieu, small saltwater fish
lièvre, rabbit (hare)
lièvre en cabessal, stuffed hare dish
limande, dab (flounder)
limande sole, lemon sole
limonade, lemonade-flavored soft drink

Limonade is a carbonated soft drink.

liqueur, liqueur
lisette, small mackerel
lit, bed (as in a bed of lettuce)
litre, liter. Wine is often served in a liter carafe, *demi-litre*
 (half-liter) or *un quart* (quarter-liter)
livarot, round, sharp, tangy cheese
Loire, this valley is one of France's wine regions along the
 Loire River
longe, loin. *Longe de veau* is loin of veal
longeole, pork sausage stuffed w/cabbage, leeks and spinach.
 A specialty in French-speaking Switzerland
lonzu, shoulder (in Corsica)
lorraine, usually braised in red wine w/cabbage
lotte, monkfish
loubine, fish similar to sea bass
lou cachat, crushed cheese
lou magret, breast of fattened goose or duck
lou mäis, corn-meal cake found in Provence

Lou means "the" in Provencal!

loup/loup de mer, sea bass. *Loup au fenouille* is sea bass grilled over fennel stalks

lou pevre, goat's-milk cheese w/coarsely ground pepper

lou piech, stuffed veal dish found around Nice

louvine, fish similar to sea bass

Lucullus, dish that contains extremely rich and/or rare ingredients. Named after a Roman general who hosted great feasts

lyonnaise, sautéed w/mushrooms and/or onions/sauce of onions, butter and white wine ("Lyon style")

macaron, macaroon. Not the sticky coconut version found at home, but two almond-meringue cookies, flavored with vanilla, chocolate, coffee, pistachio or other flavors, stuck together with butter cream

macaroni au gratin, macaroni and cheese

macédoine, mixed fruit or mixed vegetables

macédoine de légumes, mixed vegetables

macérer, to pickle or soak

mâche, a type of lettuce

macis, the outer covering of a nutmeg/mace

mache.

Mâcon, wine from Burgundy

mâconnaise, usually refers to a goat's milk cheese

macreuse, pot roast

madeleine, butter cake

madère, w/Madeira wine

magret, breast of fattened goose or duck

maigre, lean

maïs, corn

maison, house

maître d'hôtel, head waiter/sautéed in butter w/lemon juice and parsley

maltaise, orange-flavored *hollandaise* sauce

mandarine, tangerine

mange-tout, snow pea/type of apple

mangue, mango

manière, de, in the style of

mange-tout

maquereau, mackerel

means eat all

maraîchère, usually means w/various greens (market style)

marbré, marbled

marc, a strong liqueur made from distilling the residue of grapes (similar to Italian *grappa*). *Marc de Bandol* is a popular *marc* found in Provence

marcassin, young wild boar
marchand de vin, red wine and shallot sauce/wine merchant
marché, market
marée, a term used to denote fresh seafood (literally "the tide")
Marengo, à la, w/eggs
marennes, flat-shelled oysters
margarine, margarine (almost never served in Paris)
Margaux, a red wine from Bordeaux
mariné, marinated
marinière, "sailor's style" usually means w/seafood (most
    often mussels) simmered in herbs and white wine
marjolaine, marjoram. This can also refer to a layered
    chocolate and nut cake
marmelade, marmalade
marmite, food cooked in a small casserole
marquise, mousse cake
maroilles, strong, hard cheese
marron, chestnut
marrons au sirop, chestnuts in vanilla-flavored syrup
marrons chauds, roasted chestnuts.
    Served on the streets of Paris
marrons entiers au naturel, chestnuts in water
    (used in stuffing, sauces or as a vegetable)
marrons glacés, candied chestnuts
marrons Mont Blanc, chestnut purée
    and cream on a spongecake soaked in rum
massepain, marzipan
matafan, simple cake (flour, butter, milk and eggs) made in a
    skillet
matelote, freshwater fish stew/fish stew (usually eel) w/wine
    from the French West Indies. *Matelote de veau* is veal stew
    w/red wine
mauresque, a drink of *pastis* w/almond and orange syrup
mauviette, meadow lark
mayonnaise, mayonnaise
médaillon, small, round cut of meat
Médoc, red wine from Bordeaux
mélange, mixture/blend
mélasses, molasses
méli-mélo, assorted seafood
méli-mélo de légumes, mixed vegetables

Marquise... don't miss having this.

marrons ~ have never seen the appeal of these.

melon, cantaloupe

melon à l'italienne, melon w/*prosciutto*

melon d'eau, watermelon. The French call it ***pastèque***

melon de Cavaillon, similar to a canteloupe

ménagère, a basic preparation usually w/carrots, potatoes and/or
  onions (means "in the style of a housewife")

mendiants, dessert made of dry figs, raisins, almonds and nuts

menthe, mint

menthe poivrée, peppermint

menu, menu (often a fixed-price meal)

menu dégustation, set-price gourmet
  menu of specialties of the chef

Menu degustation is usually better Quality.

menu du jour, menu of the day

menu fixe, fixed-price menu

menu gastronomique, gourmet menu

menu pour enfant, children's menu

mer, sea

merda, *gnocchi* made w/Swiss chard

merenda, morning snack

merguez, spicy sausage (usually lamb)

meringues, baked shells of sweetened, beaten egg whites

merlan, whiting

merle, blackbird

Merle.

Merlot, dry, medium- to
  full-bodied red wine

merlu, a type of hake

merluche, dried cod

mérou, grouper

merveille, sugar doughnut

No thanks.

mesclun, lettuce salad of mixed greens

messine, an herb and cream sauce

méthode champenoise, sparkling wine (natural method)

mets, dish/preparation

mets selon la saison, seasonal preparation

meunière, w/parsley butter/seasoned fish floured and fried in
  butter, lemon and parsley. The word means "miller's wife"
  which refers to the flour that is used to prepare this dish

meurette, w/red wine sauce

Meursault, wine from Burgundy

miel, honey

miettes, flakes/crumbs

miel Lavan...

mignardises, *petits fours* (small fancy cookies or cakes)
mignon, tenderloin cut
mignonette, small piece of fillet/coarsely ground white pepper
mijoté, simmered
milieu de poitrine, brisket
millas, corn-meal mush
mille-feuille, light pastry w/cream filling (napoleon)
millésime, vintage
mimolette, a mild cheese
mimosa, w/chopped egg yolks
mirabeau, w/anchovies and olives
mirabelle, yellow plum/plum brandy
mireilie, à la, there are many versions
    of this cold marinade
mirepoix, vegetables cut into cubes
miroir pommes, apple-Bavarian cream dessert
miroton, slices. Can also refer to a meat and onion stew or a
    brown sauce including onions
mitonnée, a souplike dish
mixte, mixed
mode, à la, in the style of
moelle, bone/marrow
moelleux, full-bodied. This can also mean tender
moka, coffee
mollusques, shellfish
momie, thimble-sized *pastis*
montagne, de, from the mountains
Mont Blanc, chestnut meringue topped w/a "mountain" of
    whipped cream (named after the mountain peak)
montmorency, w/cherries
morceau, piece
morille, morel mushroom (a rare,
    wild mushroom w/a smoky flavor)
mornay, white sauce w/cheese
mortadelle, bologna sausage
    w/pistachios and pickles
morue, salt cod
morue en rayte, cod in red wine sauce
moscovite, a dessert made in a mold w/any number of
    ingredients/a way of preparing duck
mouclade, creamy mussel soup

[handwritten note: Mille feuille means a thousand leaves.]

[handwritten note: morceau~ mor-So]

moule, mussel
moule de bouchot, small cultivated mussel
moule d'Espagne, large sharp-shelled mussel (frequently served raw)
moule de Parques, Dutch cultivated mussel
moules à la crème, mussels in white wine w/cream
moules à la poulette, mussels in a rich white wine sauce
moules marinières, mussels simmered in white wine w/shallots
mourtayrol, chicken dish flavored w/saffron
moussaka, a Greek dish frequently found on menus in Paris. It is an eggplant, lamb and tomato casserole
mousse, a light and airy dish of whipped cream or beaten egg whites/chopped meat or fish w/eggs and cream
mousse au chocolat, chocolate mousse
mousse de foie gras, *foie gras* must have, under French law, fattened liver w/up to 20% other foods. *Mousse de foie gras* contains up to 45% other foods such as eggs, pork liver and/or truffles
mousseline, w/whipped cream/*hollandaise* sauce w/cream
mousseron, small wild mushroom
mousseux, sparkling
moutarde, mustard 
mouton, mutton
muge, mullet (in Provence)
mulet, mullet
munster, full-bodied cheese, often flavored w/caraway, cumin or anise)
mûre, blackberry
muscade, nutmeg
Muscadet, a dry, white wine
muscat, dessert wine
museau, muzzle
muscau de veau, calf's muzzle
myrtille, blueberry
mystère, cooked meringue dessert w/ice cream
nage, "swimming;" served in an aromatic poaching liquid
nantua, crayfish or shrimp sauce
napolitaine, vanilla, strawberry and chocolate ice cream
nappe, tablecloth
nappé, covered in a sauce
nature, plain

handwritten: muzzle... sounds grim.

handwritten: myrtille~ mir-tee.

naturel, plain. *Au naturel* means plainly cooked

navarin, mutton stew w/turnips

navet, turnip

nefle, small orange-colored fruit

nègre, flourless chocolate cake

neige, w/beaten egg whites (means "snow")

neufchâtel, rich, creamy cheese (a lower-fat cheese)

Newburg, lobster cooked in a sauce made of butter, cream,
    winc (or brandy) and egg yolks. Newburg is an alteration
    of Wenburg, the name of the patron for whom the
    sauce was named

niçoise, usually means w/tomatoes, anchovies, vinegar and
    black olives. Named after the city of Nice

nid d'abeilles, honey cake

nivernaise , à la, a dish w/carrots and onions

Noilly Prat, French vermouth

noir, black

noisette, hazelnut/round piece of meat

noix, nut/walnut. This can also refer to nuggets

noix d'acajou, cashew

noix de coco, coconut

noix de muscade, nutmeg

noix de pecan, pecan

noix de veau, top side of the leg of veal

non, not or no

nonats, tiny Mediterranean fish served deep fried

normande, usually means cooked w/fish, cream and mushrooms
    ("Normandy style"). This can also refer to a dish in a
    cream sauce often w/*calvados*

nougats, roasted almonds, egg whites, nuts and honey dessert

nouilles, noodles

nouilles fraîches maison, homemade fresh pasta

nouveau, new

nouveauté, new offering

nouvelle, new

noyau, pit (as in an olive pit)

Nuits-Saint-Georges, high-quality red wine from Burgundy

oeuf, egg. *Blancs d'oeufs* are egg whites
    and *jaunes d'oeufs* are egg yolks

oeuf à la coque, soft-boiled egg

oeuf à l'américaine, fried egg

Handwritten annotations:

Navarin... I'll pass.

abeille~ bee

Noisette can also mean a small cup of cafe crème.

Oeuf à la Coque— egg in the shell.

95

oeuf à la russe, hard-boiled egg served
  cold w/diced vegetables in mayonnaise
oeuf à l'Huguenote, poached egg w/meat sauce
oeuf au plat, fried egg
oeuf brouillé, scrambled egg
oeuf chemise, poached egg
oeuf Côte d'Azur, poached egg in an artichoke
  bottom
oeuf dur, hard-boiled egg
oeuf dur soubise, hard-boiled egg w/onion and cream sauce
oeuf en gelée, poached egg served in gelatin
oeuf en meurette, poached egg in a red wine sauce
oeuf farci, stuffed egg
oeuf frit, fried egg
oeuf mayonnaise, eggs and mayonnaise
oeuf mollet, soft-boiled egg
oeuf poché, poached egg
oeuf poché à la Chartres, poached egg w/tarragon
oeuf Rossini, egg w/truffles and Madeira wine. This can also be a
  poached egg w/*pâté*
oeufs à la diable, devilled eggs
oeufs à la neige, whipped, sweetened egg whites served in a
  vanilla custard sauce (means "eggs in the snow")
oeufs au lait, egg custard
oeuf sauté à la poêle, fried egg
oeufs au vin, eggs poached in red wine
oeufs d'alose, cooked fish (shad) eggs
oeufs en meurette, poached eggs w/red wine sauce from
  Bourgogne
oeufs fermier, eggs from poultry raised on a farm
oeufs pochés suzettes, poached eggs in baked potatoes
oeuf sur la plat, fried egg
offert, free ("offered")
oie, goose
oie à l'instar de visé, goose boiled and
  then fried. A Belgian specialty
oignon, onion
oignons grelots, small pickled onions
oiseau, bird
olives, olives
olives farcies, stuffed olives
olives noires, black olives

olives vertes, green olives
omble-chevalier, freshwater fish of the trout family (char)
omelette, omelet
omelette au fromage, cheese omelet
omelette au jambon, ham omelet
omelette au lard, bacon omelet

Olives Farcies.

omelette au naturel, plain omelet
omelette aux champignons, mushroom omelet
omelette aux fines herbs, omelet w/herbs
omelette brayaude, potato omelet
omelette César, omelet w/garlic and herbs
omelette complète, omelet w/ham and cheese
omelette fourée aux pommes dite à la Normande, apple
    upside-down cake
omelette landaise, omelet w/pine nuts
omelette nature, plain omelet
omelette norvégienne, baked Alaska
omelette parmentier, potato omelet
omelette paysanne, omelet w/bacon and potatoes
omelette quercynoise, cheese and walnut omelet
onglet, hanger steak
opéra, layered spongecake w/chocolate sauce
orange, orange
orange givrée, orange sorbet served in an orange
orange pressée, fresh, squeezed orange juice
oranges en rondelles, candied orange slices in orange jelly
oreilles, ears
orcillettcs, pastry puffs
orge, barley
orgeat, almond-sugar syrup
origon, oregano
orties, nettles
ortolan, small game bird

Ortolans are eaten whole, everything but the beak. They're illegal to serve.

os, bone
os à moelle, marrow bone
oseille, sorrel (an herb eaten as a leafy vegetable)
ostendaise, w/shrimp and oysters
ou, or
ouassous, large crayfish found in the French West Indies
oursin, sea urchin
pacanes, pecans (in Guadeloupe)

paëlla, saffron-flavored rice and various ingredients. There are many variations of this famous Spanish dish found on menus all over France

pagre commun, sea bream

paillard, thin, flattened piece of meat, poultry or fish fillet

pailles pommes, fried, shredded potatoes

paillettes, cheese straws

pain, bread

pain au chocolat, chocolate-filled pastry *Pain ~*

pain au lait, sweet bun *Pan*

pain aux noix, walnut bread

pain aux raisins, bun w/custard and white raisins

pain blanc, white bread

pain complet, whole-wheat bread

pain de campagne, chewy "country" bread

pain de mie, sliced white bread (sandwich bread)

pain d'épices, gingerbread/a dense spice cake w/honey

pain de seigle, rye bread

pain de son, bran bread

pain de sucre, sugar loaf

pain grillé, toast

pain noir, dark bread

pain ordinaire, French bread

Bread is buttered at breakfast but not lunch or dinner.

pain perdu, French toast. Literally, "lost bread" invented because French bread has no preservatives, thus becomes hard very quickly. The milk and eggs soften the bread

pain viennois, Vienna loaf

palaia, small sardines and anchovies

palais, cookies. *Palais de dames* are fruit cookies

paleron, shoulder of beef

paletot, skin, bone and meat of a fattened goose or duck (after th liver is removed)

palets de marrons, puréed-chestnut patties

palette de porc, pork shoulder

palmiers, palm hearts (*coeurs de palmier*). This can also refer tc a caramelized puff pastry

paloise, *béarnaise* sauce w/mint

palombe, pigeon

palourdes, clams

pamplemousse, grapefruit

Always liked that word.

panaché, mixed. *Un panaché* also refers to a drink made of half
   beer and half lemon soda

panade, thick mixture used to bind dumplings (panada)

panais, parsnip

pan bagnat, large round sandwich filled w/olive oil, onions,
   olives, tomatoes, anchovies and a hard-boiled egg. A
   specialty on the Côte d'Azur (means "wet bread").
   This is a *salade niçoise* sandwich

pané, breaded

panier, basket

panisses, chickpea-flour pancake (deep fried)

panne de porc, fat from the kidneys of a pig

pannequet, rolled, filled crêpe

papalines, orange-flavored chocolates from Avignon

papeton d'aubergines, eggplant casserole from Avignon
   (means "eggplant of the popes")

papillons, butterfly cookies. This can also refer to a type of oyster

papillote, en, baked in parchment paper

paquets, en, in packages or parcels

parfait, ice-cream dessert. Can also refer to goose, duck or
   chicken-liver mousse

parfum, flavor

Paris-Brest, ring-shaped *éclair* filled w/praline cream

parisienne, a vegetable garnish w/potatoes sautéed in butter
   w/a white sauce

parme, amberjack (in Provence)

parmentier, dish containing potatoes

part, portion

partager, to share

passe-pierre, seaweed

Passe-Tout-Grain, red wine from Burgundy

pasta, pasta. Originally from neighboring
   Italy, pasta is an important part
   of Provençal cuisine

Pastèque.

pastèque, watermelon

pastilles, hard, fruit- or mint-flavored candy

pastis, anise-flavored aperitif. This is a Provençal word meaning
   mixture. It is a summer drink. Common
   brands are Pastis 51, Pernod, Ricard,
   Granier, Prado and Henri Bardouin

pastis landais, a sweet bread dessert

patate, sweet potato
patate douce, sweet potato
pâte, pastry dough.
> This can also mean a batter or paste.
> Do not confuse this w/*pâté* or *pâtes*

pâte à choux, cream-puff pastry
pâte à foncer, shortbread crust
pâte à frire, sweet french-frying batter
pâte à pain, bread dough
pâte brisée, pie pastry
pâte d'amandes, marzipan
pâte de fruits, fruit-paste candies
pâte feuilletée, puff pastry
pâte levée, bread dough
pâte sablée, sweet pie pastry
pâte sucrée, sweet pie pastry
pâté, pâté
pâté ardennais, purée of pork in a loaf of bread
pâté de campagne, *pâté* w/a variety of meats
pâté de canard, duck *pâté*
pâté de foie de volaille, chicken-liver *pâté*
pâté de foie d'oie, *pâté* that contains at least 50% goose liver and
> up to 50% other meats

pâté de foie gras, goose-liver *pâté*. Contains at least 75% goose
> liver

pâté doré, seasoned baked pork-liver *pâté* served cold
pâté en croûte, *pâté* in a pastry crust
pâté en pot, mutton soup found in the French West Indies
pâté maison et rillettes, a slice of a loaf of ground seasoned meat
patranque, bread andbacon pancake
pâtes, pasta
pâtisserie, pastry
patranque, bread and bacon pancake
patte, foot (paw) or leg of an animal or bird
patte blanche, small crayfish
patte rouge, large crayfish
Pauillac, rich red wine from Bordeaux
paupiette, slice of veal or beef rolled around stuffing
pavé, thick slice of beef (or calf's liver)
pavé aux marrons, chestnut and chocolate cake
pavot, graines de, poppy seeds

Pâte is pastry.
Paté is pâté.
Pâtes is pasta.

Patte blanche

paysanne, à la, "country style" usually means a dish containing assorted vegetables

pays d'auge, cream and cider sauce

pays, du, from the area

peau, skin

pêche, peach

pêche melba, peaches w/ice cream and raspberry sauce

pêcheur, this term refers to fish preparations (means "fisherman")

pelardons, goat cheese

pelé, peeled

pelure, peelings

perce-pierre, seaweed

perche, perch

perdreau, young partridge

perdrix, partridge

périgourdine, à la, w/goose- or duck-liver purée and truffles

périgueux, a brown sauce w/chopped truffles

Pernod, anise-flavored aperitif

perroquet, a drink of *pastis* and mint

persil, parsley. *Persillé* means parslied

persillade, chopped parsley and garlic

pesto, see *pistou*

pétillant, slightly sparkling beverage

petit, small

petit beurre, tea biscuit

petit déjeuner, breakfast

petite friture, fried whitebait

petit four, small fancy cookie or cake

petit gâteau, small cake/cookie

petit-gris, small snail

petit noir, black coffee

petit pain, roll. *Petits pains au maïs* are made w/corn meal

petit pois, pea

petit pois de cérons, peas w/pork

petit salé, salt pork

petits farcis provençaux, stuffed vegetables of Provence

petits gâteaux, cookies

petits pois, peas

petits pois à la Normande, creamed peas

petit-suisse, creamy, unsalted cheese/cheese *beignets*

Petits Pois.

pétoncle, tiny scallop
pets de nonne, small fried pastry
pibale, small eel
pichet, pitcher of wine

Pichet —
Pee-shay

picodon, goat's-milk cheese from Provence
picon bière, beer mixed w/a sweet liqueur
pièce, piece/each
pied, foot
pied de cochon, pig's foot
pied de mouton, wild mushroom/sheep's foot
pied de porc, pig's foot
pieps et paquets, stuffed-tripe dish
pietra, chestnut-flavored beer from Corsica
pieuvre, octopus
pigeon, pigeon
pigeonneau, young pigeon
pignatelle, small cheese fritter
pignons, pine nuts/croissant w/pine nuts
pilaf/pilau, rice cooked w/broth and onions
piment, chili pepper/pimento
piment doux, sweet pepper
piment en poudre, chili powder

Piment doux

piment poivre de Jamaïque, allspice
pimprenelle, burnet (a green used in salads)
pince, claw
pineau, cognac and grape juice
pintade, guinea hen
pintadeau, young guinea hen
pipérade, omelet w/ham, green peppers, tomatoes and garlic
piquant, spicy hot
piquante, sauce of pickles or capers, shallots and vinegar
piqué, larded
pissala, fish purée used in *pissaladière*

Never warmed
up to this

pissaladière, pizza-like tart w/onions,
    black olives and purée of anchovies
    and sardines (from Provence)
pissenlit, dandelion leaves
pistache, pistachio
pistil de safran, thread of saffron
pistou, garlic, basil, nuts and olive oil sauce (known as pesto in
    Italy)/pesto soup

pithiviers, puff pastry filled w/ground almonds and sweet cream

pizza, pizza is not shared in France, is not eaten w/your
hands and will be served w/a bottle of olive oil w/hot
peppers at the bottom. The oil is to spice up your pizza.
A cheese and tomato pizza is called a ***marguerite***

pizza quatres saisons, four-seasons pizza (four toppings: ham,
mushrooms, cheese and anchovy)

pizza reine, pizza topped w/ham and mushrooms

planteurs, rum and fruit punches found in the French West Indies

plaque de chocolat, chocolate bar

plat, plate/dish

plat de résistance, main course

plat du jour, plate (special) of the day

plate, flat-shelled oyster. This can also
refer to water w/out carbonation

plateau, platter

plateau de fromages, platter of cheeses. In Normandy, this is
almost always served w/*calvados*

plat froid, cold plate

plat minceur, diet plate

plat principal (plats principaux),
main course(s)

pleurote, grey mushroom
found in the Loire Valley

plie, flounder/plaice

plie franche, flounder

plombières, vanilla ice-cream dessert
w/whipped cream and candied fruit

pluviers, plovers (small birds)

poché, poached

pochouse, fish and onion stew
prepared w/wine (from Bourgogne)

poêle, à la, fried

point, à, medium done. In France,
this means still pink

pointe, tip. ***Pointe d'asperge*** is
an asparagus tip

poire, pear

poireau (poireaux), leek(s)

poire Belle Hélène, pear w/ice cream and chocolate sauce

poirier d'anjou, pear cake

*Plat minceur.
I hope you're
just looking this
up to see what
it is, not
ordering it.*

Plie.

*A poêle is
a frying pan.*

pois, peas

pois chiche, chick-pea

pois mange-tout, snow pea

poisson, fish

poisson à grande friture, deep-dried fish

poisson d'eau douce, freshwater fish

poisson de mer, saltwater fish

poissonnerie, fish soup/fish store

poitrine, breast

poitrine d'agneau Sainte Menehould, braised and grilled lamb breast

poitrine demi-sel, slab of unsmoked bacon

poitrine de mouton, mutton breast

poitrine de porc, pork belly

poitrine de veau, veal breast

poitrine fumée, slab of smoked bacon

poivrade, brown sauce of wine, vegetables, peppers and vinegar

poivre, pepper. *Au poivre* means w/peppercorns

poivre d'Ain, flavored *banon* (cheese)

poivre d'ane, bitter, peppery herb

poivre de cayenne, very hot red pepper

poivre de Chine, mouth-numbing type of peppercorn

poivre de la Jamaïque, allspice (the main ingredient of jerk seasoning)

poivre frais de Madagascar, green peppercorns

poivre mignonette, crushed peppercorns used on steaks

poivre noir, black peppercorns

poivre rose, pink peppercorns

poivre vert, green peppercorns

poivron, bell pepper

poivron doux, sweet bell pepper

poivron épicé, hot pepper

poivron rouge, red pepper

poivron vert, green pepper

polenta, corn meal/polenta (dish of boiled corn meal, w/butter and cheese)

Pomerol, a red wine (merlot) from Bordeaux

pommade, a thick paste

pomme, apple

pomme au four, potato baked in its skin

pomme bonne femme, baked apple

pomme de terre, potato
pomme de terre brayaude, oven-cooked potato
pomme en l'air, caramelized apple slices
    served w/blood sausage
pommes à l'anglaise, boiled potatoes
pommes allumettes, very thin french fries
pommes anna, sliced potato and cheese dish
pommes boulangère, a potato and
    meat dish/sliced potatoes w/onions
pommes château, potatoes fried in butter
pommes dauphine, potatoes mashed in
    butter and egg yolks, mixed in flour
    and deep fried

Most of the time pomme refers to potato though it means apple... sorry can't be more specific.

pommes dauphinoise, potatoes baked w/garlic, cheese and milk
pommes de terre à la berrichonne, herbed potatoes
pommes de terre à l'angoumois, potato and cabbage casserole
pommes duchesse, potatoes mashed in butter and egg yolks
pommes en robe de chambre, potatoes in their skin
pommes en robe des champs, potatoes in their skin
pommes fondantes, potatoes cooked in butter
pommes frites, french fries
pommes gratinées, potatoes baked w/cheese
pommes lyonnaises, potatoes sautéed w/onions
pommes mousseline, mashed potatoes
pommes nature, boiled or steamed potatoes
pommes nouvelles, new potatoes
pommes paille, fried strips of potatoes
pommes Pont-Neuf, french fries
pommes renversées, baked caramelized apple pudding
pommes sautées, fried potatoes
pommes soufflées, puffy slices of potatoes fried twice
pommes vapeur, steamed or boiled potatoes
pompe à l'huile, sweet flat bread flavored w/olive oil
pont l'évêque, strong, flavored, semi-hard cheese (usually
    served in square blocks)
porc, pork
porc au lait, pork cooked in milk
porc aux deux pommes, pork w/potatoes and apples
porc demi-sel, salted pork
porcelet, young suckling pig
porchetta/porketta, an Italian dish of roast, stuffed suckling pig

Pommes frites, one of the miraculous joys of France.

porc salé, salted pork

Porto, port

porto, au, w/port

port-salut/port du salut, mild, soft, buttery cheese

portugaises, a type of oyster

potable, drinkable

potage, soup (usually thick)

potage à la crème de coco, cream-of-coconut soup found in the French West Indies

potage au cerfeuil, soup of chervil and other herbs. A specialty in the Ardennes region of Belgium

potage bilbi, fish and oyster soup

potage bonne femme, potato and leek soup

potage cancalais, fish soup

potage Crécy, carrot soup

potage crème normande, cream of fish soup

potage cressonière, watercress soup

potage cultivateur, soup w/mixed vegetables and pork

potage d'Auvergne, lentil and potato soup

potage du Père Tranquille, lettuce soup

potage du Barry, cauliflower soup

potage Longchamp, soup featuring peas

potage nivernaise, carrot soup

potage parmentier, leek and potato soup

potage portugais, tomato *potage*

potage printanier, vegetable soup

potage Saint-Germain, split-pea soup

potage soissonnais, haricot-bean soup

potage velouté, creamy soup

pot-au-feu, stew of meat and vegetables

pot-de-crème, mousse or custard dessert

potée, boiled pork (or beef) w/cabbage

pothine de boeuf, beef braised w/*calvados*. The *pothine* is a cast-iron casserole in which this dish is cooked

potiron, pumpkin

Pouilly-Fuissé, dry white wine from Burgundy

poularde, capon/fatted chicken

poularde Sainte-Hélène, chicken w/dumplings

poule, hen

poule au pot, stewed chicken w/vegetables

poule au riz, hen served w/rice

potage.

NOT crazy about jellied meat.

poule d'Inde, turkey hen

poule faisane, pheasant

poule farcie en daube à la berrichonne, boned, stuffed chicken in jelly.

poulet, chicken

poulet basquaise, chicken w/sweet peppers and tomatoes ("Basque style")

poulet Biarritz, chicken in white wine

poulet.

poulet chasseur, chicken usually w/mushrooms and white wine. This can also be chicken in tomato sauce

poulet créole, chicken in a white sauce (often spicy) and served w/rice

poulet de Bresse, free-range, corn-fed chicken

poulet de grain, corn-fed chicken. Sold in shops with a special ring around its "foot" to prove they are authentic.

poulet de Saint-Astier, chicken stew

poulet fermier, free-range chicken

poulet Marengo, chicken cooked in white wine w/tomatoes, garlic, mushrooms and shallots. Said to be the chicken dish served to Napoleon after the battle of Marengo in 1800

poulet rôti, roast chicken

poulpe, octopus

pourboire, tip

poulpe.

pour/à emporter, to go/take out

pourpier, purslane (a green used in

pousse-pierre, seaweed

poussin, spring chicken

praire, clam

praline, caramelized almonds

premier cru, denotes a high-quality wine

pré-salé, lambs that graze on salt meadows

pressé, fresh squeezed

presse, à la, pressed

pression, draft beer.
À la pression means from the tap

primeur, early season or spring fruits and vegetables

Prince-de-Galles, stuffed w/*pâté*

printanière, à la, w/spring vegetables

prisuttu, cured ham from Corsica

prix, price

prix fixe, fixed price

prix net, service is included

profiteroles, little cream puffs filled w/ice
    cream and covered in chocolate sauce

Profiteroles ~ food of the gods.

provençale, à la, w/garlic, onions, herbs and tomatoes
    ("Provence style"). Provence is one of
    France's wine-growing regions and, of course,
    one of the world's best-known and
    loved tourist destinations

prune, plum

pruneau/pruneau sec, prune

pudding, custard/pudding

puits d'amour, pastry filled w/custard

pulenta, chestnut-flour bread from Corsica

purée, strained fruit or vegetables.
    En purée means mashed

purée de pommes de terre, mashed potatoes

pyramide au chocolat, chocolate pyramid filled w/chocolate
    pieces and sauces, whipped cream and butter

quartiers d'orange glacés, caramelized orange sections. A
    dessert found on menus in Provence

quart, un, on a menu this denotes a quarter-liter of wine

quatre-épices, a blend of four spices
    (nutmeg, cloves, ginger and
    white pepper)

quatre-quarts is like pound cake.

quatre-quarts, a cake made from
    four ingredients – eggs, flour,
    butter and sugar – of equal weight.
    A specialty in Brittany

quenelle, dumpling

quenelles de foie de veau, calf's-liver dumplings. A specialty in
    Luxembourg

quetsche, small plum/liquor made from plums

queue, tail

queue de boeuf, oxtail

quiche, egg tart w/vegetable, seafood or meat filling

quiche au fromage blanc, bacon and white cheese *quiche*

quiche lorraine, *quiche* w/cheese, bacon and onions

râble, loin of rabbit

râble de lièvre, saddle of rabbit

racasse, scorpion fish

108

raclette, cheese heated until it begins to melt. The melted part is scraped off and placed on a warm plate to be eaten w/boiled potatoes, pickles and pickled onions. This can also refer to melted cheese on a *baguette*

radis.

radis, radish

radis noir, large black radish

ragoût, stewed/meat stew

raie, ray/skate (fish)

raifort, horseradish

raisin, grape(s)

raisins.

raisins de Corinthe, currants

raisins de table, dessert grapes

raisin sec, raisin(s)

raïto, red wine, tomato and onion sauce

ramequin, small cheese tart or a small casserole

rancio, dessert wine

râpé, shredded/grated. *La râpée* is a creamed-potato pancake

rascasse, fish found in the Mediterranean (scorpion fish)

ratatouille, eggplant casserole

rave, root vegetable

ravigote, vinegar dressing (w/herbs and shallots)

ravioli, ravioli. Common in Nice and all of the French Riviera

reblochon, soft, strong cheese

refroidi, chilled

à la reine...
of the
queen.

régional(e), from the region/local

reine, à la, w/mince meat or poultry

reine-claude, small green or yellow plums (greengage)

reinette, fall and winter apple

religieuse, *éclair* pastry. This pastry got its name because it looks like a nun in her habit

rémoulade, mayonnaise sauce

renversée, turned out of its cooking container

repas, meal

Rhône, this valley is one of France's wine regions (located in South Central France) and known for its white and red wines

rhubarbe, rhubarb

rhum, rum

Ricard, anise-flavored aperitif

Richelieu, à la, w/tomatoes, bacon and potatoes

rigotte, goat cheese

rillettes, highly seasoned meat baked in its own fat (potted meat)

rillons, pork belly
ris, sweetbreads
ris d'agneau, lamb sweetbreads
ris de..., sweetbreads
ris de veau, veal sweetbreads (the pancreas of a veal calf)
rissole, pastry/meat or fish patty
rissolé, fried until brown and crisp
riz, rice. *Crème de riz* is rice flour
    (very finely gound rice)
riz à l'impératrice, rice pudding
riz basquais, spicy rice
riz complet, brown rice
rizotto, risotto
riz pilaf, rice boiled in bouillon w/onions (rice pilaf)
riz safrané, saffron rice
riz sauvage, wild rice
robe des champs, en, in its skin
Robert, a brown sauce w/onions, white wine and mustard
rocambole, a member of the onion family
rognon, kidney
rognonnade, veal loin
rognons blancs, testicles
rognons de veau à la liégeoise, roast veal kidneys
romarin, rosemary
romsteck, rump steak
rondelle, round slice
roquefort, blue cheese
roquette, arugula (rocket)
rosbif, roast beef
rosé, rosé. This can also refer to rare meat
rosette, dried sausage/small round piece
Rossini, a dish that includes *foie gras* and truffles
rôti, roast/roasted
rouelle, a slice cut at an angle
rouelle de veau, veal shank
rouge, red
rouget, red mullet
rouille, spicy sauce of peppers, garlic and tomatoes
rouilleuse, red garlic mayonnaise
roulade, rolled slice of meat or fish w/stuffing/"Swiss roll"
    dessert w/cream or jam stuffing

Handwritten margin notes:

ris – ree
riz – ree
Don't get em mixed up.

Rognon ~ runyun

Pass on the entire Rongum selection

Rouget.

roulé, rolled
rouleau, roll of...
roussillonnade, grilled sausage and mushroom dish
roux, flour and butter mixture (used to thicken sauces or soup)
rouzoles, crêpes filled w/bacon and ham
rumsteck, rump steak
sabayon, creamy dessert of wine, sugar, egg yolks and
    flavoring/cream wine sauce
sablé, shortbread cookie
saccharine, saccharin
sachet de thé, tea bag
safran, saffron
saignant, very rare
saindoux, pork fat
Saint-Amour, red wine from Beaujolais
Saint-Emilion, red wine form Bordeaux
Saint-Estèphe, red wine from Bordeaux
Saint-Germain, w/peas
Saint-Honoré, cake w/cream
Saint-Hubert, sauce w/bacon and chestnuts
Saint-Jacques, sea scallop
Saint-Julien, red wine from Bordeaux
Saint-Marcellin, goats' or cows' cheese w/a smoky flavor
Saint-Raphaël, quinine-flavored aperitif
Saint-Paulin, mild, semi-soft cheese
Saint-Plerre, John Dory fish (a firm-textured, white fleshed fish
    w/a mild, sweet flavor and low fat content)
saison, season
salade, salad
salade antiboise, salad usually w/fish, capers and green peppers
salade au bleu, salad w/blue cheese (and frequently walnuts)
salade au chapon, salad served on toast rubbed w/garlic
salade aux noix, green salad w/walnuts
salade cauchoise, ham, potato and celery salad
salade chiffonnade, shredded lettuce and sorrel
salade composée, chef's salad
salade d'Auvergne, salad w/blue cheese dressing
salade de boulghour, bulgur wheat salad
salade de crudités, chopped vegetable salad
salade de fruits, fruit cocktail
salade de gésiers, green salad w/gizzards

St. Emilion~ personal favorite.

Chapon refers to the toast.

salade de liège, bean and potato salad. A specialty in Belgium

salade de museau de boeuf, marinated beef headcheese

salade de saison, seasonal salad

salade de tomates, tomato salad

salade folle, mixed salad usually w/green beans

Salade folle ~ crazy salad

salade lyonnaise, *hors d'oeuvre* of seasoned meats in an oil, shallot and vinegar dressing

salade mélangée, mixed salad

salade mêlée, mixed salad

salade mesclun, mixed greens

salade mixte, mixed salad

salade multicolore, salad w/radishes, peppers, egg, cucumber, corn and basil

salade niçoise, salad usually w/tomatoes, anchovies or tuna, potatoes, vinegar and black olives (served as a main course)

salade panachée, mixed salad

salade paysanne, salad w/eggs and pieces of bacon

salade russe, diced vegetables in mayonnaise

salade simple, green salad

salade verte, green salad

salade wallonie, warm salad w/lettuce, bacon and fried potatoes. A specialty in Belgium

salaisons, an hors d'oeuvre of olives, anchovies and/or herring

salé, salted

salicorne, algae used as a condiment

salmis, roasted game or poultry

salpicon, stuffing w/sauce

Salpicon — like the word and the concept!

salsifis, salsify (oyster plant)

Sancerre, white and pale, light-bodied red wines from the Loire Valley

sandre, pike

sandwich, sandwich

sandwich au fromage, cheese sandwich

sandwich au jambon, ham sandwich

sandwich au saucisson, dried-sausage sandwich

sandwich aux rillettes, *pâté* sandwich

sandwich crudités, lettuce and/or chopped vegetable sandwich

sang, blood

sanglier, wild boar

Sanglier. A specialty in the Ardennes.

112

sans, without
sans arêtes, boneless
sans peau, skinless
sarcelle, teal (river duck)
sardine, sardine
sarrasin, buckwheat
sarriette, summer savory (an herb)
sartando, small fried fish w/hot vinegar
sartenais, hard, strong cheese from Corsica
sauce, sauce/gravy/salad dressing
sauce à la crème, cream sauce
sauce aurore, a white sauce w/tomato purée
sauce aux câpres, a white sauce w/capers
sauce bigarade, orange sauce
sauce bretonne, egg, butter and mustard sauce
sauce café de Paris, cream, mustard and herb sauce
sauce catalane, tomato, orange and garlic sauce
sauce gaillarde, seasoned mayonnaise
sauce mornay, cheese sauce
sauce poulette, mushroom, egg yolk and wine sauce
sauce soubise, onion sauce
sauce Suzette, orange sauce
sauce veloutée, creamy soup/white sauce (*roux* mixed w/poultry, fish, veal or mushroom stock)
sauce vinot, wine sauce
saucisse, sausage
saucisse à l'ail tiède, garlic sausage (served warm)
saucisse à la navarraise, sausage w/wine and sweet peppers
saucisse de Francfort, hot dog/frankfurter
saucisse de Strasbourg, beef sausage
saucisse de Toulouse, fresh pork sausage
saucisson, dried sausage
saucisson à l'alsacienne, poached sausage w/horseradish sauce
saucisson à la lyonnaise, poached sausage w/potato salad
saucisson chaud de Lyon en croûte, sausage w/cubes of fat and baked in pastry
saucisson de Lyon, dried seasoned sausage
sauge, sage
saumon, salmon

*Saucisse ~
Sausage like
bratwurst
Saucisson ~
Sausage like
Salami*

Sauge. 113

saumon de l'Atlantique, Atlantic salmon

saumon fumé, smoked salmon

Saumur-Champigny, light-bodied red wine from the Loire Valley

saupiquet, spicy cream sauce w/bread crumbs

saupiquet des amognes, ham w/spicy cream sauce

sauté, sautéed

Sauternes, a fruity white dessert wine

sauvage, wild

Sauvignon de Touraine, white wine from the *Sauvignon Blanc* grape

savarin, spongecake topped w/rum and cream

Savoie, one of France's wine-growing regions

savoyarde, flavored w/cheese. *À la savoyarde* also can refer to a vermouth and cream sauce

scampi, prawns

scarole, escarole, a salad green (a type of *endive*)

scotch, scotch

sec, dry/straight

séché, dried

seiche, large squid/cuttlefish

seiches farcies, cuttlefish stuffed w/a mixture of sausage and the meat of cuttlefish tentacles

seigle, rye

sel, salt

sel-épicé, salt spiced w/basil, nutmeg, cloves, cinnamon, peppercorns, bay leaves and coriander

sel gemme, rock salt

sel gris, coarse rock or sea salt

selle, saddle of meat, generally the loin roast

selle anglaise, saddle of meat

sel marin, sea salt

selon arrivage, on a menu, this means the dish depends on availability

selon grandeur/selon grosseur, price paid by the size or weight

sel raffiné, refined salt

semoule, semolina flour

sériole, amber jack, a type of fish

serpolet, wild thyme

serran, perch

service compris, service included

service non compris, service not include
serviette, napkin
s.g., abbreviation for price paid by the size or weight
sherry, sherry
sirop, syrup
sirop de sucre d'érable, maple syrup
smitane, cream, wine and onion sauce
socca, *crêpe* made w/chickpea flour served on the Côte d'Azur
soissons, white beans
soja, soy
sole, sole
sole normande, sole in a butter, onion, mushroom, white wine, cream and *calvados* sauce
son, bran
sorbet, sherbet
soubise, onion sauce
soubise-aurore, onion and tomato sauce
soucoupe, saucer
soufflé, soufflé (beaten egg whites w/various ingredients baked in a mold)
soufflé à la reine, soufflé w/poultry or meat
soufflé au Grand Marnier, soufflé w/orange liqueur
soufflé Rothschild, vanilla-flavored fruit soufflé
soupe, soup
soupe à l'oignon gratinée, French onion soup
soupe au pistou, vegetable and noodle soup (soup w/pesto found in the South of France)
soupe corse, Corsican soup of vegetables and herbs simmered w/a ham bone
soupe de montagne, Corsican soup of vegetables and herbs simmered w/a ham bone
soupe de poisson, fish soup
soupe paysanne, Corsican soup of vegetables and herbs simmered w/a ham bone
soupe pêcheur, fish soup
spaghetti, spaghetti
spats, small fish of the herring family
spécialité, specialty
spécialité de la maison, house specialty
spécialité du chef, chef's specialty
spécialités locales, local dishes

Sorbet.

steak, steak

steak au poivre, steak topped w/crushed peppercorns. *Steak au poivre vert* is steak in a green-peppercorn sauce and *steak au poivre rouge* is steak in a red-peppercorn sauce

steak frites, steak and french fries

steak haché, hamburger

steak tartare, raw hamburger or chopped beef (usually topped w/a raw egg)

stockfish, niçoise spicy fish stew

stufatu, Corsican stew w/pasta

succès au pralin, meringue cake w/almonds

sucettes, lollipops ("suckers")

suchi, sushi

sucre, sugar

sucre candi, candy sugar

sucre de canne roux, brown sugar

sucre filé, spun sugar

Sucre filé is found adorning Croquemboche.

suprême, chicken-based sauce/breast of chicken or game or fillet of fish w/an unusual combination of ingredients

suprême de volaille, chicken breast. Usually a boned chicken breast in a creamy sauce

sur commande, to your special order

surgelé(s), frozen food

surlonge, beef chuck roast

sus, en, in addition. *Boisson en sus* means drink not included

Suze, an aperitif flavored w/gentian, an herb

tablier de sapeur, grilled breaded tripe

tagine/tajine, stew (lamb, veal or chicken) w/vegetables. This spicy stew is a specialty in North Africa (especially Morocco). Also a clay cooking vessel

Tagine

tanche, the freshwater fish tench

tapenade, mixture of black olives, olive oil, lemon juice, capers and anchovies (a spread from Provence)

Tanche.

tarama, mullet-roe spread

tartare, chopped raw beef/in a salad, this refers to a mayonnaise-based sauce

tarte, pie/tart

tarte à l'oignon, onion and cream tart

tarte alsacienne, apple and custard tart

tarte au citron meringuée, lemon meringue pie

tarte au fruit, fruit tart

tartelette, small tart

tarte tatin, upside-down apple tart. Legend has it that this tart was "created" when the Tatin sisters (who operated a restaurant) put the tart in the oven and left for church. They discovered their mistake, turned it upside down and served it.

tarte tropézienne, yellow cake w/custard filling (created by a Polish baker in 1955 in St Tropez)

tartine, open-faced sandwich (half baguette w/butter)

tasse, cup

Tavel, rosé wine from the Côte du Rhône region

The luscious-sounding Tartine buerré is nothing more than buttered bread.

tendre, tender

tendre de tranche, round steak

tendron, breast

tendron de veau, veal breast

terrine, *pâté*/prepared in an earthenware dish

terrine de campagne, pork and liver *pâté*

terrine de légumes, ground and seasoned vegetable loaf

terrinée, caramel-rice pudding

tête, head

tête de veau vinaigrette, calf's head w/vinegar and oil dressing

teurgoule, caramel-rice pudding

thé, tea

thé au lait, tea w/milk

Not on your life!

thé citron, tea w/ lemon

thé glacé, iced tea

thé nature, tea w/out milk

thon, tuna

thon mirabeau, tuna cooked in eggs and milk

thym, thyme

tian, a dish (usually rice, vegetables and cheese) cooked in an oval-shaped earthenware dish used on the Côte d'Azur

tian de Saint-Jacques et légumes provençal, sea scallops on a bed of chopped vegetables

tiède, lukewarm

tilleul, herb tea

timbale, cup. *En timbale* means meat, fish or fruit in a mold

ti punch, rum, lime and sugarcane syrup drink found in the French West Indies

'Ti means petit

tisane, herbal tea

toast, toast (little pieces of crispy bread)

tomate, tomato. This also is the name for a drink of *pastis* mixed w/grenadine

tomates à la provençal, baked tomatoes stuffed w/bread crumbs, garlic and parsley

tomates concassées, roughly chopped tomatoes

tomates farcies, tomatoes stuffed w/seasoned bread crumbs

tomme (or tome) au marc, the crust of this smooth and creamy cheese is made of grape pulp. Also known as *fondu aux raisins*

tomme (de Savoie), soft, mild cheese

tonique, tonic

tonneaux en chêne, oak barrels

topinambour, Jerusalem artichoke

tortue, turtle

tortue véritable, turtle soup

toulousaine, usually means served w/sweetbreads or truffles ("Toulouse style")

tourain, bread and garlic soup

tourin bordelais, French onion soup (usually w/bread on the bottom of the bowl)

tournedos, round cut of prime steak

tournedos Rossini, *tournedos* served w/Madeira wine sauce and served w/*foie gras* and/or truffles

tourta da blea, Swiss chard pie

tourte, pie

tourteau, large crab

tourte aux blettes, sweet tart of eggs, cheese, raisins, pine nuts and chard

tourte du jour, savory pie of the day

tourtière, pastry filled w/prunes and/or apples. Also the name for a cooking dish

tourton, pastry filled w/prunes, apples, spinach and garlic

tout compris, everything is included in the price

tout épice, allspice

tranche, slice. *Tranché* means sliced

tranche grasse, sirloin tip

tranche napolitaine, slice of layered ice cream

travers de porc, spareribs

treipen, black pudding and sausages w/potatoes

très, very

trifle, trifle

tripe, tripe

tripe à la luxembourgeoise, tripe
specialty found in Luxembourg

Remember the general rule about Tripe... don't.

tripes à la mode, tripe in butter, onions and *calvados*.
A popular dish in Normandy

tripes à la mode de Caen, tripe baked w/calf's feet

tripes à la mode narbonnaise, tripe in tomato sauce

Triple Sec, orange liqueur

tripoux, mutton tripe

trompettes des morts, wild mushrooms

tronçon, large slice of meat or fish

trouchia, trout. In Provence, this refers to an omelet

truffat, potato-cream pie

truffe, truffle. *Truffé* means w/truffles. Truffles are extremely
expensive wild fungi that grow around the roots of trees.
They must be "sniffed out" by pigs or dogs. *Truffes* also
refers to chocolate truffles

truffettes dauphinoise, chocolate truffles

truite, trout

truite à l'ardennaise, Belgian dish of
trout cooked in a wine sauce

Truite.

truite au bleu, poached trout

truite meunière, trout in a parsley and butter sauce

truite saumonée, salmon trout

ttoro, Basque mixed-fish dish

tuile, almond cookie

turbon, ingredients cooked in a ring mold

turbot, turbot, a fish

turbotin, small turbot

vacherin, mellow Swiss cheese

vacherin glacée, baked meringue dessert

valençay, goat's-milk cheese

Vallée d'Ange, w/cooked apples and cream (named after a region
in Normandy)

vanille, vanilla

vanneau, small bird

vapeur, steamed

varié/variés, assorted

veau, veal

veau Marengo, veal w/garlic, tomatoes, white wine and cognac
végétarien/végétarienne, vegetarian
velouté, creamy soup/white sauce
    (*roux* mixed w/poultry, fish,
    veal or mushroom stock)
velouté d'asperges, creamy white asparagus soup
venaison, venison
ventre, stomach/belly
ventrèche, salted and seasoned pork belly
vénus, clam
verdures, green salad vegetables
verjus, the juice of unripened grapes
vermicelle, tiny, thin noodles used in soup
vermouth, vermouth
vernis, large clam
verre, glass
vert, green/a sauce of spinach,
    mayonnaise and herbs
vert-pré, watercress garnish
verveine, the herbal tea lemon verbena
vessie, cooked in a pig's bladder
viande, meat
viande séchée, thin slices of cured beef
viandes froides, cold meats
vichy, w/glazed carrots
vichyssoise, cold leek and potato soup
vieille, old
vieille cure, wine-distilled liqueur
vieille prune, plum-based *eau-de-vie*
vierge beurre, a simple butter sauce w/lemon juice, salt and pepper
vierge huile d'olive, virgin olive oil
vieux, old
vigneronne, sauce w/grapes and wine
vigne, sarments de, vine cuttings used w/grilled foods
vin, wine
vinaigre, vinegar
vinaigre balsamique, balsamic vinegar
vinaigre de vin, wine vinegar
vinaigrette, generally a salad dressing
    of vinegar, mustard, herbs and oil

Handwritten notes:

Verjus is sometimes used instead of vinegar.

Une verre de vin rouge

Vielle cure means remedy... An excuse to drink...

Vin is pronounced Van with just a hint of the 'N'.

in blanc, white wine

in chambré, wine served at room temperature

in cuit, sweet dessert wine

in Délimité de Qualité Supérieure (VDQS), denotes a local
  wine made according to strict standards

in de maison, house wine

in de paille, straw wine w/a strong flavor and aroma

in de pays, wine guaranteed to originate in a certain region
  ("country wine")

in de table, table wine

in de xérès, sherry

in doux, sweet wine/dessert wine

in doux naturel, naturally sweet wine

in du pays, local wine

in gris, pink wine

in jaune, a dry whiite wine from Jura *The French don't*
fill their glasses
in liquoreux, sweet wine *more than*
halfway
in mousseux, sparkling wine

in nouveau, new wine

in ordinaire, table wine

in rosé, rosé wine

in rouge, red wine

in sec, dry wine

iolet de Provence, braid of garlic

iolette, crystallized violet petals

ivant/vivante, alive/living *Volaille ~*
Voe - Lie.
odka, vodka

olaille, poultry

ol-au-vent, puff pastry filled w/fish, meat and/or sweetbreads

vaterzooi, chicken or fish poached in a sauce w/vegetables. A
  Belgian specialty

vaterzooi de poulet, chicken poached in a sauce w/vegetables

vhisky, whisky

Villiamine, a pear brandy

érès, sherry

aourt/yogourt, yogurt

vorne, a dry Swiss white wine

este, citrus zest

este de citron, lemon zest

este de citron confits, candied lemon zest

este d'orange, orange zest

ewelwai, onion and cream tart from Alsace

Descriptions of restaurants listed here can be found on the page number following each listing.

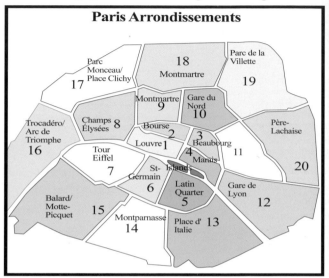

Paris Arrondissements

1. Louvre/Les Halles
Café Marly 45
Le Fumoir 22
Le Grand Véfour 29
Juvenile's 24
Lavinia 41
Ô Chateau 41
Spring 28
Verjus Bar à Vins 30
Willi's Wine Bar 34
2. La Bourse
Le Art Source 35
Coinstot Vino 35
Frenchie 22
Le Grand Colbert 33
Legrand Filles et Fils 41
Aux Lyonnais 33
Noglu 43
Osteria Ruggera 24

Le So 43
3. Beaubourg/Marais
Au Bascou 19
Chez Janou 21
Le Hangar 23
Le Petit Marché 25
Le Taxi Jaune 28
4. Marais/Ile-Saint-Louis
L'Ambroisie 29
L'Ange 20 19
Bistrot de L'Oulette 20
Bofinger 31
Café Beaubourg 44
Chez Marianne 32
Gaspard de la Nuit 23
Ma Bourgogne 33
Le Petit Bofinger 31
Le Potager du Marais 43
Sorza 28

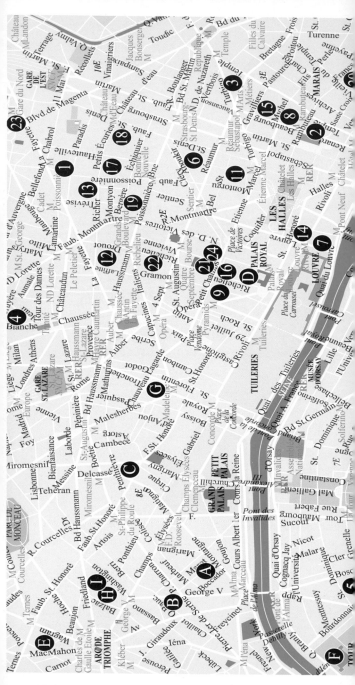

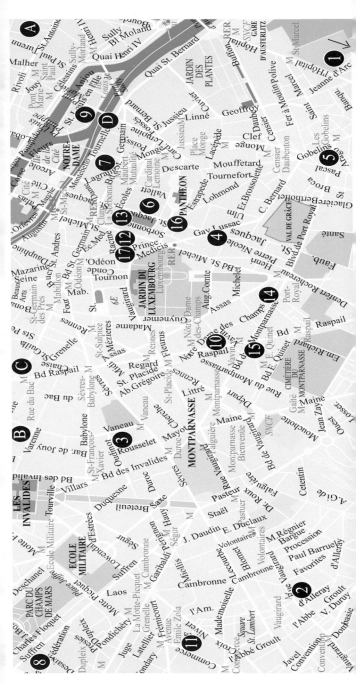

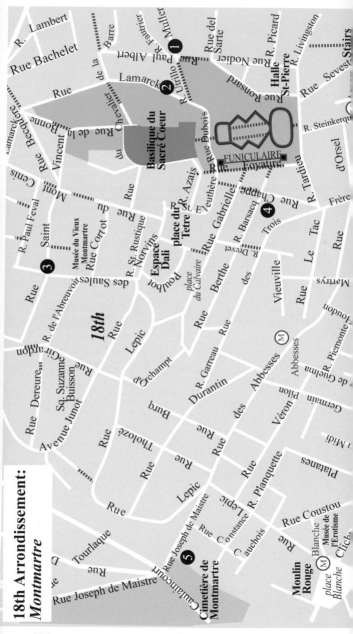

18th Arrondissement: *Montmartre*

R. Lambert

R. Bachelet

Rue Bachelet

Rue Lamarck

Lamarck

de la

Barre

R. Paul Feutrier

Rue Paul Albert

R. Urillo

Muller

Rue del Sarte

Rue Nodier

Rue Picard

R. Livingston

Halle St-Pierre

Rue Ronsard

Rue Sevestre

Stairs

Rue de la Bonne

Rue du Chevalier

Basilique du Sacré Coeur

R. Dubois

R. Steinkerque

Rue Vincent

Mont Cenis

R. Paul Feval

Rue Saint

Rue du

Musée du Vieux Montmartre

Rue Cortot

Rue St. Rustique

Espace Dali

FUNICULAIRE

Rue Foyatire

R. Tardieu

d'Orsel

Frère

Rue St. Eleuthère

Rue St. Azais

place du Tetre

Rue Norvins

Rue Poulbot

Rue Gabrielle

Rue Chappe

R. Drevet

R. Barsacq

Trois

Le Tac

Rue

Rue des Saules

R. de l'Abreuvoir

place du Calvaire

Rue Berthe

Rue des

Vieuville

Rue

Martyrs

Rue Girardon

Rue Dereure

Sq. Suzanne Buisson

Avenue Junot

Rue Lepic

Rue d'Orchampt

R. Garreau

Rue Durantin

Rue Burq

Rue des

Rue Véron

Germain Pilon

Abbesses

R. Piemonte

de Guelma

Houdon

18th

Rue Tholozé

Rue Lepic

Rue Constance

R. Planquette

Platanes

Midi

Rue Tourlaque

Rue Joseph de Maistre

Rue Caulaincourt

Rue Joseph de Maistre

Cimetière de Montmartre

C. Cauchois

Rue Coustou

Rue Blanche

Museé de l'Erotisme

Clich

Moulin Rouge

place Blanche

① ② ③ ④ ⑤

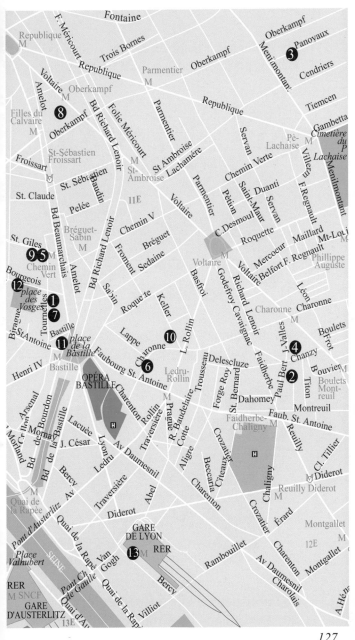

Informative, Opinionated, Funny

The best menu translator/restaurant guides available!
Handy, pocket-sized ... a must for all travelers.

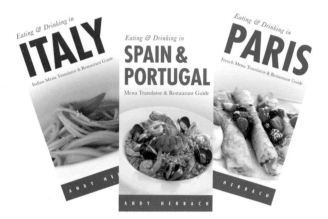

For more restaurants, wine bars, wine shops, and food
shops, check out the *Wining & Dining* guides!

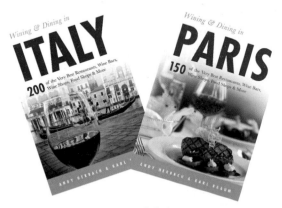

www.eatndrink.com
Published by Open Road Publishing
Distributed by Simon & Schuster